FIFTEEN THOUSAND PIECES

A Medical Examiner's Journey Through Disaster

MIROLAND IMPRINT 44

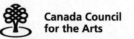

Canada Council
for the Arts

Conseil des Arts
du Canada

ONTARIO ARTS COUNCIL
CONSEIL DES ARTS DE L'ONTARIO
an Ontario government agency
un organisme du gouvernement de l'Ontario

Canadä

Guernica Editions Inc. acknowledges the support of the Canada Council
for the Arts and the Ontario Arts Council. The Ontario Arts Council
is an agency of the Government of Ontario.
We acknowledge the financial support of the Government of Canada.

FIFTEEN THOUSAND PIECES

A Medical Examiner's Journey Through Disaster

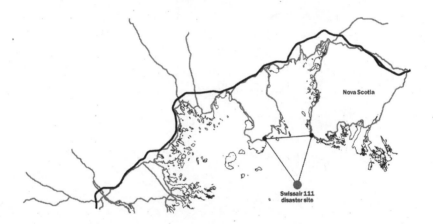

Nova Scotia

Swissair 111
disaster site

Gina Leola Woolsey

MiroLand
p u b l i s h e r s

MIROLAND (GUERNICA)
TORONTO • CHICAGO • BUFFALO • LANCASTER (U.K.)
2023

Guernica Founder: Antonio D'Alfonso

Connie McParland, Michael Mirolla, series editors
Gary Clairman, editor
David Moratto, cover design and interior design

Guernica Editions Inc.
287 Templemead Drive, Hamilton, ON L8W 2W4
2250 Military Road, Tonawanda, N.Y. 14150-6000 U.S.A.
www.guernicaeditions.com

Distributors:
Independent Publishers Group (IPG)
600 North Pulaski Road, Chicago IL 60624
University of Toronto Press Distribution (UTP)
5201 Dufferin Street, Toronto (ON), Canada M3H 5T8

First edition.
Printed in Canada.

Legal Deposit—Third Quarter
Library of Congress Catalog Card Number: 2022951963
Library and Archives Canada Cataloguing in Publication
Title: Fifteen thousand pieces : a medical examiner's journey through disaster /
Gina Leola Woolsey.
Names: Woolsey, Gina Leola, author.
Identifiers: Canadiana (print) 20230133150 | Canadiana (ebook) 20230133215 |
ISBN 9781771838115 (softcover) | ISBN 9781771838122 (EPUB)
Subjects: LCSH: Butt, John (John C.) | LCSH: Medical examiners (Law)—
Nova Scotia—Biography. | LCSH: Gay men—Nova Scotia—Biography. |
LCSH: Swissair Flight 111 Crash, 1998—Biography. | LCSH: Coming out
(Sexual orientation)—Nova Scotia. | LCGFT: Biographies.
Classification: LCC RA1025.B88 W66 2023 | DDC 614/.1092—dc23

for Michael, my love
1966–2018

Contents

CHAPTER ONE: **PLANE DOWN** 1

CHAPTER TWO: **MY MORBID CURIOSITY** 8

CHAPTER THREE: **A DEATH IN THE FAMILY** . . . 13

CHAPTER FOUR: **SHEARWATER** 23

CHAPTER FIVE: **PATHOLOGY** 32

CHAPTER SIX: **PRESERVER** 45

CHAPTER SEVEN: **HEROES** 56

CHAPTER EIGHT: **HABEAS CORPUS** 65

CHAPTER NINE: **HOMECOMING** 75

CHAPTER TEN: **IDENTITY** 86

CHAPTER ELEVEN: **THINGS FALL APART** 95

CHAPTER TWELVE: **MEMORIAL** 107

CHAPTER THIRTEEN: **DISASTER TRAINING** . . . 116

CHAPTER FOURTEEN: **MEMENTO MORI** 127

CHAPTER FIFTEEN: **BODY OF SECRETS** 138

CHAPTER SIXTEEN: **ACCOLADES & CONDEMNATIONS** . . . 148

CHAPTER SEVENTEEN: **DISCLOSURE** 160

CHAPTER EIGHTEEN: **LOST & FOUND** 169

CHAPTER NINETEEN: **WRONGFUL DEATH** 180

CHAPTER TWENTY: **PATHFINDER FORUM** 193

CHAPTER TWENTY-ONE: **CLUB DEAD** 206

Acknowledgements 223

About the Author 225

CHAPTER ONE

PLANE DOWN

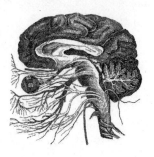

September 2nd, 1998

THE PHONE ON the bedside table rings minutes before 11 p.m. on a rainy Wednesday night. It's a woman from his office.

"I've just had a call from the Halifax Rescue Coordination Centre. A plane's gone down somewhere off the Aspotogan Peninsula."

Dr. John Butt, Nova Scotia's Chief Medical Examiner (ME), and his two dogs are ready for bed. Deputy and Ben, golden retrievers, flank their master, ready for the night's watch.

"What is it?" He knows what she's going to say—a small craft, or a local carrier flight.

"It's an international flight. It's Swissair."

The information doesn't go straight to the action center in his brain. His plausibility muscle bats away the news so his mind has a minute to rev the mental engines.

"I think there's some room for double checking on this."

Dr. Butt, a forensic pathologist with over thirty years of experience, lives across the bay from the peninsula, about half an hour's drive from his office in Halifax where he leads the medically focused aspects of Nova Scotia's death investigations.

He'd only returned home a short time ago, after a long day in

1

court, two hours away in New Glasgow. His testimony had been postponed and the impatient doctor was forced to wait on the sidelines for his turn to give evidence of murder. The victim, a cab driver, had been strangled with a ligature placed from behind, and asphyxiated. It was an upsetting case; a deadly robbery that netted the two young assailants a handful of loose change. The Chief ME was determined to have his moment on the stand for the poor man, despite the waiting game.

As he drove home, a dark sky overtook the milky twilight. On grey fall days in Nova Scotia, the clouds crouch low over the rocky coastline, as if conspiring with the sea to swallow houses and towns. It's a different feeling than the expansive semi-circle sky of John's hometown in Alberta, where the air is dry and the land gently dips and rises toward the far-flung horizon. The people here, they're different too.

His office calls back. It's confirmed. A Swissair commercial plane has gone down off the Aspotogan Peninsula.

John's internal alarm sounds, igniting the flow of adrenaline through limbs and vital organs. The buzzing won't be far behind. At sixty-three, and after three decades of work in his field, John is no stranger to large-scale disasters. An international flight carrying possibly hundreds of people is proving difficult to imagine. *How? Where? Why?* The panic in his belly threatens, spreading its searing fingers, pushing blood from vital organs to the extremities, flushing his face and scattering his thoughts.

John drags a suitcase out of the walk-in closet and throws it open on the bed. He moves back and forth between his clothes and the bag, a repetitive motion to occupy the alarming thoughts while his brain works to find the logical next steps. *I should be back in a day or three*, he thinks, trying to compile a mental list of what one needs when heading off to deal with an international disaster.

Jan and Geoff, John's best friends in Nova Scotia, live across the road. In a few days, when John runs out of clean clothes, he'll ask Jan to bring him more. John, always dapper in his dress, gives her a list—the grey suit, the blue shirt with French cuffs, the soft yellow tie. But Jan is colour blind and her choices are mismatched attempts to follow his instructions. In the years to come, they will laugh at her fumbles, laugh at how John struggled to put together a sombre but stylish outfit to address the families or the television cameras. The laughter will help them remember, and forget.

It takes him half an hour to gather his thoughts and finally zip the suitcase closed. By this time, the horrific news has travelled a circuitous route through his defence mechanisms and become true. He must keep his thoughts orderly and make the adrenaline work in his favour to stay ahead of the emotions. He never wants to hear that dreaded buzzing sound in his head again.

The dogs need minding. He calls his other neighbours, Frank and Shirley, a friendly couple just down the road. Shirley answers the phone, even though it's after 11 p.m. Of course they'll take the dogs, she tells him, don't worry about it one bit. She soothes his jagged nerves with her reassuring voice.

Shirley is an angel. This isn't the first time she's come to his aid. When he moved across the country, from Calgary to Halifax, Shirley greeted him with neighbourly warmth. In Alberta, it's customary to invite newcomers into your home for a meal or a cup of cheer. John finds the people on this coast friendly and earnest, but somehow not welcoming. He has trouble feeling connected to new people who don't extend dinner invitations or host parties. Shirley seemed different, and she invited him and his dogs into her life right away. It didn't take long for them to discover their shared friends. As it turns out, Shirley and her husband, Frank, lived in Alberta too, and they have common acquaintances back in Calgary.

With Jan and Geoff across the road, plus Frank and Shirley close by, John feels reasonably content in his seaside saltbox. Their three houses sit atop a small spit of land across the bay from the Aspotogan Peninsula. John's picture window overlooks St. Margaret's Bay and the arm of land that hugs the opposite shoreline. Had the neighbours been scrutinizing the dark sky that night in the minutes before impact, they might have seen the doomed aircraft on its final trajectory into the ocean.

After the call to Shirley, John checks the dogs off his mental list. Time to pass on the news. He needs to rally the troops and call the commander. His staff consists of one highly competent administrative assistant named Linda, two Nurse Investigators and one part-time file clerk. He starts with Linda.

* * *

A loud noise rips through the still air above the house. Trinkets and framed family photos shake on wooden shelves around the perimeter of the living room. Linda, a stout, working mom, and her giant-sized husband are spending a few minutes with the TV and their teenage daughter before heading up to bed.

"Oh my heavens! Do you hear that plane? Next they'll be landing in our living room," Linda says. She has to be up early the next morning to attend a workshop in Liverpool with her boss and several RCMP members. It's her job to keep things going, to smooth out the rough edges of Dr. Butt's communication style, and to keep him cooperating, especially when the RCMP are involved. She needs her rest.

The parents leave their daughter with the TV and head up to bed, both fast asleep within minutes, the sound of the too-close plane quickly forgotten. Sometime after 11 p.m., the ringing phone wakes her.

"There's a plane down somewhere off the Aspotogan Peninsula," Dr. Butt says.

"What do you mean? Like, in the water?" Linda is groggy.

"I don't know exactly, but I believe so."

"What kind of plane?" Linda enters her short period of denial. Surely, if it's true, it must be a small plane. It must be a manageable tragedy. How can it be anything else?

"A big passenger plane. A Swissair plane." John stabs at her disbelief.

"Oh my heavens!"

"You have to meet me at the office right away. You'll have to get up and come in right now. I need to call Emergency Measures. You'll need to call the RCMP and coordinate with them. We'll have to gather up—"

"Ok, listen," she says, interrupting his flurry of instructions. "I'm hanging up the phone and I'm coming to meet you at the office."

"Or, I should call the RCMP. You call Emergency Measures. We'll need to coordinate with everyone." John continues his rapid fire.

"Listen." She interrupts him again. "Now, listen. I'm going to hang up so I can get dressed and I'll be on my way."

Linda knows how to deal with her boss. She respects him for his intelligence and everything he's done to bring the Nova Scotia Medical Examiner's office to its current state of efficiency. Before Dr. Butt, there were so many problems. Now everything is done the same—all the investigations, all the paperwork, all the files throughout the province are part of one, unified system. The Medical Examiner relies on rural family doctors and hospital pathologists to visit distant crime scenes and do lab work. Before Dr. Butt, the ME office often waited over a year for pathology results. Government funding was minimal and Linda worked alone with the previous Chief ME. Dr. Butt changed all that.

Other aspects of her boss, in Linda's opinion, aren't as admirable. He's a micro manager who worries over everything. He needs to be in control and it causes a great deal of friction between the ME's Office and some of the RCMP. He's often fighting with one colleague or another, and Linda is called on to make things OK. The toughest test of her skill is about to start.

Linda's daughter bounds up the stairs to her parents' room. "Mom, mom! It's on TV. A passenger plane went down off Peggy's Cove!"

Within minutes, clear in her mission and direction, Linda is dressed and heading toward Halifax.

* * *

Robert Conrad wakes to the sound of the nightly news on his living room television. He must have fallen asleep. The regular broadcast has been interrupted and a voice cuts through his semiconscious haze. A commercial airliner is down in the St. Margaret's Bay area, somewhere near his home.

Bob Conrad has raised his family on the tuna he's fished from the waters of St. Margaret's Bay. It is his extended yard, his home, and his workplace. The house that shelters him from the wild seasonal shifts of coastal atmosphere rests next to the shore of the bay. Waves lapping on the rocks can be heard from his kitchen table.

People must be out there right now, lost in the dark water, clinging to life. The need to find the crash site, to find survivors and pull them from the sea, takes Bob hostage. Within minutes, he is kneeling at the bedside, telling his wife that a plane has crashed into water nearby and he needs to take the boat out and help however possible.

"But, Bob, what about our rule?"

"No, no. It'll take you too long to be ready. I can't wait. Listen on the VHF and you'll know what's happening. You'll know I'm OK."

Bob rushes out the door and down the road to North West Cove, a thumbprint notch of shelter on the jagged edge of the peninsula where his boat is moored. At the dock, journalists hover, pecking at the other fishermen who've felt the same pull to help. The reporters with their camera crews want rides out to the crash site. Bob sets off without passengers, despite the rule he never go out by himself, and despite requests from the boat-less reporters on the dock. For some reason, he needs to do this alone.

* * *

David Wilkins, an ophthalmologist from California, and his wife fly from their home in Loma Linda to Seattle for a visit with friends. They've already said goodbye to their youngest child, nineteen-year-old Monte, at the airport when he left to attend university in France. He's flying to New York, then transferring to a flight bound for Geneva where he'll spend a little time on his way to school. It's bittersweet. The kids have all left the nest and the parents accept their new freedom with equal measures of nostalgic longing and excitement. They're a happy and devout family ready for the next stage of independent togetherness.

* * *

John loads the car with his carefully packed bags. The sky is overcast and a thin rain blackens the pavement. The air smells of moldering leaves and wet stone. At the end of the driveway, he turns left onto Norvista Lane, away from his friends and beloved dogs. The drive to the main road leading to the city is hilly and narrow with twists and turns that trace the shape of the landscape. Scrubby underbrush and thin trees cling to the shoulders of the pavement. At the intersection of the coastal country road and the highway, he wonders which way to go. The instinct to head toward the crash site, where he imagines soon-to-be heroes are charging to the rescue, pulls at John. But what help could he give there? And where? *I don't even know where the bloody thing went down! Better to be sensible,* he decides, and turns the car toward town, his office, and the disaster manual he wrote years ago.

CHAPTER TWO

MY MORBID CURIOSITY

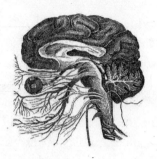

MATT WAS HIS best friend. He wasn't ready to say goodbye. "He's a wonderful, wonderful dog," John said at least once every time I'd visit. A gentle golden retriever, Matt had a habit of bringing his stuffed animal to the door to greet guests, head low, almost shy, tail wagging, like a child showing off a favourite toy. When he was especially pleased, he'd howl.

Matt had been diagnosed with cancer. Chemo had extended his life, but John was torn about the therapy. He was brought up on the prairies, where animals were rarely treated like humans. I called John after I saw the group text about Matt's demise. I was worried.

"I'm not morbid about it at all," he told me. "I'm okay."

"You've been preparing for this, I suppose." I was relieved. He sounded well.

"It's difficult in the evening. We always went to the park after supper and I'd chat with the other dog people. But I've kept myself busy." He went on to list a dizzying array of activity for a twenty-four-hour period.

How can a man of eighty-three have so much more energy than me? I wondered. In the five years we've been friends, he's travelled more, and had more adventures than I have managed to experience during my forty-nine years. He certainly knows how to embrace living. Perhaps it comes from his intimacy with death.

I met John while attending my first *Quarterly Dinner Group*—a three-hour affair with cocktails, dinner, and an intellectual or political speaker during dessert—in the dining room of the Vancouver Lawn and Tennis Club, or Van Lawn as it's known to the locals. The venue is classic men's club: chic with plenty of wood and leather. I'm one of the few women in attendance. At each meeting, one by one, we stand to introduce ourselves and give updates on our professional lives, or any news we may wish to share. Many of these men have been attending for twenty years. Most of them shoot for laughs. John is no exception. At my first dinner, his opening sentence grabbed my attention.

"I'm Dr. John Butt, and you don't want to meet me professionally, because if you did, you'd be dead." He stood for a few beats, rocking gently back to front, heel to toes, waiting for the ripple of laughter to die down before he went on with his update. He reminded me of a sartorial Alfred Hitchcock.

I leaned over to my husband, Michael, and whispered, "I need to meet that guy."

I'm drawn to people who can handle death. Acceptance seems like some kind of enlightenment. Here was a man who'd spent his life with corpses and tragedy. More, he'd gone through med school, and then *chosen* to further educate himself with a specialization in forensic pathology, and a life working with death. I wanted to find out why. I was sure the answer was important.

During cocktail hour at a subsequent dinner group evening, I was formally introduced to the doctor by my accommodating better half. In our brief but dense conversation, John and I established that we are both Alberta-born, irreligious (this is important for two Albertans) food fanatics who enjoy wine, and have a healthy respect for nature. He made me laugh. His questions reminded me of our shared experience with prairie patriarchy.

Minutes into our meeting he asked, "What does your father do?"

After I'd given my family credentials, I asked my brave question. "I'm fascinated by your work, Dr. Butt. Would you consider being interviewed for a profile?"

I went to his office for our first one-on-one meeting a few weeks after that dinner. We sat in a glass-walled boardroom and I asked embarrassingly naïve questions.

"What made you want to become a forensic pathologist?"

I'd done some digging before our meeting. He'd essentially created the Office of the Chief Medical Examiner for the Government of Alberta in the seventies. For seventeen years afterward, he was at the head of medical-legal jurisprudence in the province. After his tenure as the Chief ME in one of Canada's wealthiest provinces, John moved across the country to the Maritimes, where he served as Nova Scotia's Chief ME. Four years, and one life-altering catastrophe later, he moved to Vancouver and dedicated himself to his own consulting agency. Dr. Butt's experience with disasters piqued my morbid curiosity: two train wrecks, one in a busy London suburb, the other on a winding stretch of track in the Canadian wilderness; a deadly tornado that mowed a path through Alberta's northern capital; and a devastating plane crash in Nova Scotia that taught him, finally, what he was truly capable of giving.

I wanted my semi-obsession with death to lead me somewhere. I thought we'd talk about life in the presence of bloody organs stopped by some unknown cause, or of limbs severed from unknown owners, or stomach-churning putrefaction, and most of all, of great loss.

He swatted away the questions and even looked confused that I wanted to talk about death or anything philosophical. I felt silly. He was a scientist after all. I'd have to come at it from another direction.

"Why don't you tell me a bit about yourself?" I forged ahead. My notebook was open, pen poised, but no recorder. It was too soon.

"I'm just home from a terrible holiday trapped in a car with my cousin and his wife. He was very, very rude to her."

We chatted on about how the whole fiasco had left him so upset—he couldn't stop turning the thing over and over in his head.

The cousin-altercation led to further talk of his family; a difficult relationship with his mother, a yearning for more time with his father, and a lack of connection with his own children. He spoke candidly from the start. I had assumed I would be presenting my case to him, convincing him to share with me, but that wasn't so. He was ready to tell his story.

When I asked him why he wanted to expose himself to close scrutiny, he confessed to vengeful thoughts. Despite his apparent motivation to punish people for making his professional life difficult, his stories came around, again and again, to the impossibilities in his personal life. His complexity multiplied, as did my interest.

John told me he'd been approached to write his story in the past, after the Nova Scotia crash. No one had the right attitude. Maybe they reminded him too much of the press, greedy for gore. Was that what I wanted, too? I had to be clear with my intentions.

"Why me?" I asked him.

He seemed flummoxed by the question. "You're in the dinner group, and starting out with your writing career. I want to give you a leg up."

"Well, I appreciate that, but I can't promise anything." I was nervous. It was already clear from our conversation that he had a perfectionist streak, a controlling nature, and a giant but delicate heart. There was also this sensitive and caring side that came out in his expressions, inflections, and gestures. I didn't find out until much later that John had a penchant for nurturing careers in those he found worthy. It was obvious to me he carried a great wound, and I understood that. As a result, John was a walking, talking, emotional lightning rod, and I understood that, too.

Then he said the thing that grabbed me. "I can talk to you. I feel like I can tell you things."

By September, I was driving to John's house on Friday evenings. We sat for at least two hours at a time. I posed one question after another while the tape recorder's red light glowed between us. I watched his gestures and admired his manly hands, long and broad with straight phalanges and solid bundles of carpal bones. He wore a gold signet ring on his left hand. I thought, *The things those hands have touched.*

We talked a great deal about the Swissair disaster in the early interviews. The flight from New York, bound for Geneva, spiralled into the ocean near Halifax, the capital city of Nova Scotia. Two hundred and twenty nine people were on that flight and not one survived. In the aftermath, a community of kind-hearted folks was thrown onto the world stage, and tormented by the immense tragedy for months, even years. Mourners who lost loved ones travelled from distant continents to witness the scene. As the Chief Medical Examiner, John inadvertently became the lodestone for the families' grief. It was a pivotal time in his life.

I kept questioning his career path. Why, and how, does someone become a forensic pathologist? I thought there would have been an epiphany moment, or a lifelong desire, but when is the plot of one's life so obvious? John held a secret at his centre.

In the handful of years since John and I met, I have travelled across the country interviewing his colleagues, friends, family, and foes, and gathered what feels like an endless pile of details: divorce proceedings, court transcripts, Black Friday, the Hinton rail disaster, Swissair, and more. My journey morphed from death investigation to something resembling an archeological dig. I was slowly exposing the bones of a public life lived in hiding. I've spoken personally to the people given a point of view in these pages. It became difficult to reconcile a single truth. But is there ever such a thing when it comes to a complicated human life? Their stories were all varying degrees of different. Some people refused to be interviewed but were impossible to leave out. Some names were changed, by request, for privacy.

This is John's story.

CHAPTER THREE

A DEATH IN THE FAMILY

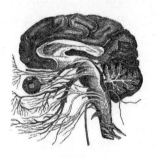

June, 1958, International Waters, Pacific Ocean

HMCS ANTIGONISH HAD left Hilo Harbor, Hawaii a few hours prior to the call from the Naval Command Office in Esquimalt, British Columbia. By the time the Captain changed course, the closest port was Pearl Harbor. It had been seventeen years since Japanese torpedo and fighter planes landed a devastating attack on the naval station at Pearl Harbor and brought the US into the war; thirteen years since Enola Gay dropped Little Boy on Hiroshima, and Bockscar delivered Fat Man to Nagasaki. WWII had ended and the cold war gripped the psyche of a freshly post-nuclear world. Mike Wallace interviewed Aldous Huxley for rapt home viewers. TV cameras rolled as the serious men discussed Huxley's new collection of essays, *Enemies of Freedom*. Communism was the threat. Russia had the bomb. Men returned home from WWII and women were fighting to hold their places in the workforce. Feminism was on the lips of prepubescent girls soon to flaunt mini skirts and stage bra burnings. It was a brave new world.

Lieut. John Butt, a young man of twenty-three, stood at attention in his Captain's quarters where he'd been summoned for a private conversation. His slender build accentuated his height, and his dark, closely shorn hair formed a widow's peak above his forehead, like his mother's. He looked quite a bit like her.

"Lieutenant, we're sending you home," the Captain told him.

John listened, but didn't respond or react. He stood silently, a cutting figure of manhood clothed to perfection in a custom uniform.

"I'm sorry to tell you that your mother is gravely ill, Lieutenant. I've ordered the ship to shore so you can disembark."

John was serving for the summer on *HMCS Antigonish*. In 1952, he'd been accepted to a prestigious University Naval Training Division straight out of high school. His buddy was doing it, and the perks were good. It meant that John could be away from home, and his mother, for most of the summer. It wasn't easy to get accepted, but he had the right pedigree and good grades. He did well in the program, and fit nicely into an officer's leadership role as a lieutenant.

John's father, Jack, had been a Navy man. Jack was born in 1899 to Lily and Percy Butt in London, England. Tragically, Percy had thrown himself in front of a subway train in London when Jack was a child. Lily and her children struggled to stay housed and fed after the suicide. In 1915, at sixteen years old, Jack enlisted in the Royal Navy. World War I was underway with Britain entering the fray in August of 1914. Leaving danger aside, Jack saw an opportunity to get away from home and the daily drudgery of poverty. Years later, his son followed suit and used the Navy to escape his own family dynamic.

At the age of seven, John had found his dad's wooden trunk of sea-time relics in the basement. There was a .22 calibre breach-loading pistol with bullets in the chamber, a fascinating toy for the young boy. He felt the danger associated with the weapon and knew he didn't want to get caught touching it, so he only handled it on rare occasions. The uniforms drew his attention most—white, single-breasted, stiff cotton jackets with tight, stand-up collars, and white cotton trousers. He loved to imagine himself in a crisp uniform and cap, travelling the world on a grand ship. Spending time with these artifacts from his father's past became a touchstone escape for young John. Joining the Navy on an officer's path was a dream come true.

Cadet John Butt was made Sub-lieutenant Butt in 1955. Young officer cadets in training became his charges. He was responsible for their paper work, their appearance, and their discipline. Along with the added responsibility, he felt a certain added status. All the smartest looking officers ordered uniforms custom made at Gieves, an expensive Bond Street tailor in England. John chose to do the same. His dark, double-breasted jacket and pants were the finest wool, and thick gold braid twice encircled the cuff of each sleeve. John was handsome in a boyish way. He had a round face that filled with childish mischief when he smiled under the black peak of his officer's cap. Being well turned out for a living suited him to a Bond Street T. He often thought of giving up medical school and having an officer's career in the Navy.

His mother, however, knew John's future. He was going be a doctor. She had established this fact early on. Isobel Butt was serious about life. She was a no nonsense lady on a mission to educate. Born Isobel MacLean Lewis in 1905 to George and Margaret Lewis, John's mother was a proper English woman with a pragmatic approach to child rearing. Her father, George Lewis, was a devout High Anglican who worshipped daily at a church on Gore Street in Vancouver. He ran a strict home and spent his little free time reading or attending meetings of the Freemasons. Isobel's mother, Mrs. Margaret Lewis, was a Victorian-era lady who knew the rituals of a proper English tea, though she was born on a Canadian island in the Pacific Ocean. Mrs. Lewis also believed there was no place for emotional outbursts in a proper home. Life at the Lewis household was Dickensian. Adults went about with a stiff upper lip, and children were seen but not heard.

Isobel met Jack Butt in 1932 when she was a schoolteacher in Vancouver. Jack was working for the Marconi Company at that time. He had a post as the wireless radio operator aboard Canadian Pacific Steamships running tourist cruises up Vancouver Island to wild places on the northern tip where carved totems and centurion trees dominated the landscape. In the spring of 1933, Isobel and Jack were married in Vancouver. Victorian prudence hung about the era like an old shawl. Personal independence movements struggled to shrug it off. Vancouver City Council had recently passed a bylaw allowing men to go topless on city beaches. The Great Depression was the real benchmark of the times. Two provinces over, Saskatchewan was a dustbowl, three years into a drought that punctuated the economic misery for many farmers. Family homesteads were abandoned because there was nothing left to eat, nothing left to do. The Temperance Movement had fallen and the United States finally ended prohibition, crippling the Canadian rum-running industry with the flourish of a pen. Across the Atlantic, Hitler had been named Chancellor of Germany.

Jack and Isobel started a family soon after marriage. John Clulow Butt was born on September 6, 1934 in Calgary, Alberta. Jack had left the life at sea and landed a job as a travelling salesman with Procter & Gamble in Alberta. His sales territory kept him away from the family during the week, or for weeks at a stretch, but he was a loving father to little John when he was home.

Like most little kids, John loved getting into bed with his parents in the morning for a snuggle or a game of pillow fort, which his dad played with great enthusiasm. But his mother didn't like any roughhousing or messing about, and she didn't make forts or play games. She said to John when he climbed on her, "Don't touch my breasts, I'll get cancer." He didn't really know what she meant at the time, but he knew it was bad.

It had been twenty years since her words made their first impression, but they were with him still. Despite his understanding of science, and three years of medical school, he couldn't shake her ominous premonition. Was he somehow responsible for his mother lying in a hospital bed dying of breast cancer?

When he was home from university for the Thanksgiving holiday, Isobel had told him in her matter-of-fact style that she'd had a mastectomy and the procedure had left her terribly disfigured. It was a great shock to John and he felt the need to do something helpful, so he spoke with the pathologist over slides of his mother's breast tissue. The biopsy specimens outlined disfigured lymph nodes and a very bad prognosis. He knew then that she was terminal. Later, at the office with his mother's surgeon, John stepped into adulthood.

"Look, I'd like you to promise me something," John said to the surgeon. "Don't tell my father the prognosis."

"I don't think I can do that, John. Why don't you want me to tell him?"

"It's just … it's going to be so rapidly fatal anyway."

"I still don't think I can do that."

⌒ "He knows it's cancer, but in my opinion, he doesn't need to know this," John said, as definitively as possible, and left it at that. He assumed the surgeon would likely tell his father. He was wrong.

The last leg of John's journey from Hilo Harbour to Vancouver was spent on a bus. The trip was a long and slow. He had too much time to think. He worried over his little sister, wondering how she was coping with the impending loss of their mother.

Susan MacLean Butt was born in April of 1946 when John was eleven years old, but she didn't arrive at the Butt household until mid summer that year. Susan was adopted. John didn't know exactly why his parents chose to adopt a child. His mother was in her early forties, busy with her volunteer work and keeping up the home with an absent husband. John was quite jealous of any other children, as he felt that he never had enough of his dad's time for himself. Maybe if he had been more athletic, his dad would have shown him more attention. Maybe if he were smarter. Maybe if he had been a girl. It seemed to John that little girls had a way with his father that he just couldn't master. When he asked his mother why they were adopting a child, she quickly ended the conversation with a blow to his heart. "I can't have more kids because having you almost killed me."

Why couldn't he focus on the good times? John asked himself while the bus lumbered heavily toward his hometown. *Why did his mother torment him so?* And now that she was leaving him, he didn't want her to go. He didn't want his dad to be alone or his little sister, only twelve, to grow up without a mother. He was glad to live away from

Isobel, but he still wanted her there in her mother place, doing her mother things. Despite his efforts to resurrect happy memories, the painful old movies in his mind played on.

John thought back to when he was fourteen. It was 1948 and the rolling foothills of Alberta were showing their buried riches as the oil boom spread through the countryside. Calgary was flourishing. Industry leaders chose the city for their headquarters. Strong religious currents, a do-it-yourself attitude, and plenty of oil money, made Alberta into Canada's version of Texas. Men in cowboy hats with pressed shirts and fancy boots walked the city streets. They opened doors for ladies and used "Ma'am" liberally. The women dressed well, never leaving the house without hat and gloves. Downtown Calgary was the most cosmopolitan place in the province.

John had spent the morning babysitting a young girl who was staying with the family. His mother gave him bus money and told him to take the girl downtown and entertain her with some window-shopping. They went to the toy section at Eaton's department store. A ride-on train was setup on a track running around the aisles. Kids were lined up to ride for a few cents, so John used some change from the bus fare to pay for the girl. He'd have gone himself, but he was a teenager, too big for the fun at hand. John loved trains. He even dreamed of becoming a steam-locomotive engineer. Anything that travelled captured his attention. Ships and planes were favourites, too. Later that day, John had plans to meet his best friend, Alex, and ride out to the air station to look at planes. He was so looking forward to chumming around with his best pal.

"Where is my change?" his mother demanded after John and his charge returned home.

He lied. It felt like the only thing to do. Her tone was accusing, so he must have something to hide. "It must be in my jacket pocket. I'll have a look," he said, sliding from his chair at the table where they sat eating lunch. His mother followed him down the hall to the coat closet by the door. The rest of the family stayed seated, trying to ignore the growing tension.

John made a play of searching his pockets. "I must have lost it."

He tried to look innocent. He knew the lie wasn't going to hold. He saw it in her face.

"What do you mean you must have lost it?"

"I spent it on a train ride. She, she wanted to go for a ride, so I thought it would be OK."

Isobel slapped him across the face. "I'll teach you to lie to me! How dare you!"

He turned away, trying to fit between the coats in the closet and pad his head from her blows. He was almost man-sized. Isobel had to reach up to hit him on the head, her intended target. At the end of the beating, John was grounded and bawling uncontrollably. The worst part was missing his date with Alex. It was an extra embarrassment to explain over the phone and between sobs that he wasn't allowed out.

After the long bus ride, Lieut. Butt arrived home in Calgary for his final goodbye to the mother he never knew how to please. Mrs. Bulmer, Isobel's sister, and Mrs. Lewis, John's maternal grandmother, were waiting for him.

"Why is your father so shocked that your mother is dying? Surely the doctors knew she was terminal after her mastectomy? Look how quickly she's deteriorated!" Mrs. Bulmer's was fuming at her nephew.

"I told the doctor not to tell him," John admitted sheepishly.

"You did what? How could you do such a thing? It's not your place to make such decisions!" His aunt continued to berate him while his grandmother stood off to the side, nodding in agreement. They made him feel small, again, just as his mother had so many times before.

John escaped to Isobel's bedside as soon as he was able. When he arrived at her room in the Holy Cross Hospital, there were two giant bouquets; one bunch from the officers aboard *HMCS Antigonish,* the other from the crew. He was briefly overcome with emotion, but managed to control himself before anyone saw his facial contortions. Isobel herself might have cuffed him for being a sissy had she been privy to his suffocated fits of feeling. But she was in a coma. Her skin had the telltale yellow tinge of jaundice from her body's vital organs' slowing momentum, headed toward stillness. He thought he wanted to tell her that he loved her. He was sure he would have. The late afternoon light faded, casting long shadows up the walls. Her death hovered close by and its looming presence frightened him.

When John returned home after the short vigil at the hospital, his aunt and grandmother were making demands. "Well. Where is Isobel's will? I think that is the best place to start," Mrs. Bulmer said.

"I don't believe Isobel has a will," John's father replied.

"That is simply not possible. Isobel was a responsible woman. It just is not possible that she does not have a will, is it mother?" Mrs. Bulmer looked at her mother, who bobbed her head dutifully.

The women took to pulling apart the closets, rooting through the storage boxes and demanding access to any other places, such as safe deposit boxes, where one might store a will. Jack insisted that Isobel had no will, but was helpless to stop the invasion of privacy. His wife was dying. John was furious at the intrusion. He wanted to protect his dad from this insulting process, but felt helpless.

The invasion ended when Mrs. Bulmer pulled a mink stole from its hiding spot where Isobel had packed it away for the summer.

"Look mother, it's the mink! I'm quite sure Isobel wants me to have this. I'm quite sure her will states it, wherever it is." With that, the search was over.

John thought of Susan. He thought of what she might have of her mother after. He thought of how little she knew. The last time Susan had seen their mother, Isobel had a suitcase in her hand. She had acted as if she were off to visit someone far away. No one told Susan what was happening. It wasn't considered proper. Little girls needn't know about death.

John felt the overwhelming emotions threatening to take hold again, to take him down. He needed to talk to someone with compassion. His family took pride in keeping everything clamped down tight, so he went to the doctor who lived across the back alley. The man was a family friend and had been their GP for years. When he got there, he broke down. He sobbed and stuttered his anguish through the tears while the kindly doctor listened and consoled. It was an enormous relief, but it didn't last long. Mrs. Bulmer was waiting again for John with another scolding at the ready.

"Where have you been?"

John felt the familiar fear rise again from the pit of his stomach. "I was just having a visit with Doc across the way. I wasn't gone long."

"How can you be off worrying about your self when you should be here with your father and your sister. Honestly, don't you know how to be a man?" Mrs. Bulmer always had the last, cutting word that put an end to discussion.

Isobel died two days after John returned home. He wasn't at her bedside when she passed. Families were meant to show their love in brief stints during visiting hours, and otherwise stay out of the way. After her death, John was tasked with collecting her things from the hospital. As he stepped through the doors of Saint Mary's, he heard the cries of a baby's birth and thought, *One life ends and another begins*, then imagined his mother's spirit flying into the baby's body. But he didn't believe in spirits, or heaven and hell. He didn't believe in anything like that. He was a scientist.

Two men in a Packard limousine arrived at the Butt house the next day. They wore outdated mourning attire and spoke in hushed voices with hands clasped at their hearts. They asked for things. Jack chose the blue brocade dress that sister Janet had given as a gift. He found a photo of his wife, vital and alive, to guide the undertaker's hand. Then the grieving husband and his son were escorted to a funeral home on 4th Street.

The Butt men stood in a room full of caskets while the funeral directors waited below stairs. A system for allowing the families privacy was in place. Each coffin bore a detachable sign. The mourners were to bring the sign associated with their choice downstairs whenever they were ready. No rush.

John handed the chosen sign to Mr. Holloway, the funeral director. "That's a very respectable decision," Holloway said in a solemn tone. The remark irked John. *What the hell does he mean by that?*

The family viewing before the funeral was held in a small chapel.

John didn't linger over his mother's body. She was fully made-up, with curled hair, lipstick, and a satin pillow under her head. It was creepy. At least Susan wasn't there to see what they'd done to her no-nonsense mother.

Once Isobel's remains were dispatched and the ceremonies over, Mrs. Lewis and Mrs. Bulmer concluded Jack was not capable of raising Susan on his own, and Susan was soon sent to an all-girls boarding school in Vancouver. The family was blown apart. Isobel, however volatile, had been their nucleus. Without her strong force, they had no direction. Jack was bereft and alone, Susan sat crying in a dorm hundreds of miles from her family, and John lost his way. He was headed into fourth year medicine, about to realize his mother's dreams for him, but she was gone. Had he buried his medical ambition in that respectable coffin along with Isobel's painted corpse?

CHAPTER FOUR

SHEARWATER

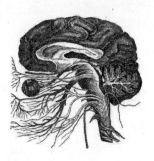

A disaster is an incident involving at least six fatalities.
—Mass Fatalities Peacetime Emergency Operation Plan

SOMETIME AFTER MIDNIGHT, the Coast Guard finds evidence of the plane's crash site. Jet fuel hangs heavy in the air and slicks an expanse of choppy water a few miles beyond the mouth of St. Margaret's Bay. John and Linda are in Halifax at the Office of the Chief Medical Examiner in the QEII Health Sciences building on the edge of the Dalhousie University campus. It's a tiny operation compared to the one he left in Alberta, where his facilities consisted of two custom-designed buildings, one in each of the province's major cities. Both the Edmonton and Calgary offices were fully staffed and equipped with the latest tools for death investigation. The Nova Scotia ME's office consists of one suite in Halifax, comprised of two dingy rooms, and tenuous privileges at the hospital morgue.

John focuses on collecting his necessary tools, most importantly the disaster appendix from the *Medical Examiner's Handbook*, which he wrote during his tenure as Chief ME in Alberta. He's not new to multiple-death scenarios. Shadowing his first mentor, working to solve the "why" of a train wreck involving forty-nine fatalities, marked the start of his career in forensic pathology. Since then, he's seen two other large-scale disasters. Each has changed him a little; made him softer, and stronger.

* * *

Linda gathers notebooks, pens, forms, phone numbers of government offices, RCMP contact lists, and information on any forensic pathologists from her desk in the outer office. In her mind, she runs through all of the things they need. They'll need help, and she's sure that's going to be a problem.

In all her years working as an administrative assistant for medical examiners, none of her bosses have had a smooth time with the RCMP. A big part of Linda's job is greasing the wheels of the powerful men around her so they'll all work together. *They're like a bunch of kindergarten kids*, she thinks. The Deputy Minister assigned a special liaison, an RCMP inspector named Pat McCloskey, to handle communications between the RCMP and the ME's office. Usually, McCloskey's gentle demeanour is enough to mollify Dr. Butt, but not always. Sometimes, Linda has to get tough to keep her boss in line.

Once, when Dr. Butt refused to talk to the RCMP guys after a fight about something or other, she marched into his office and shook his desk with a commanding hip check.

"I just had a call from the RCMP."

Dr. Butt looked back at his papers and mumbled something dismissive.

"You can't be acting like that," Linda said. "Do you realize how crazy you sound?"

More mumbling. He appeared to be ignoring her, but she didn't let it go.

"You're having a meeting with them this afternoon and you're going to behave." That was it. She turned and left his office. Later that day, the meeting went off according to Linda's plan, and under her watchful eye, with Dr. Butt playing his part.

Linda has never been afraid of saying it like it is. She does it all the time. Without her and McCloskey, things might grind to a halt around here. And now, a plane crash somewhere out on the water. With Dr. Butt and three other people making up the entire staff, Linda knows they're going to have to work hand-in-hand with the RCMP for heaven knows how long. They still don't have the passenger manifest, or know anything about the plane.

It's too quiet in the office, all things considered. It's well after midnight. *Maybe there are survivors and the emergency staff is still busy with the rescue?* She can only hope.

* * *

Bob Conrad heads toward his fishing grounds, past the mouth of St. Margaret's Bay, beyond the iconic lighthouse at Peggy's Cove on the eastern shore of the bay and the beachside town of Bayswater to the west. These are rich fishing waters and Bob knows them well. He's heard the scuttlebutt on the VHF radio. Local fishermen are out, each wave sharing what they know with the next before speeding away over dark waters, flying their hearts as flags.

Bob clears the curves of weather-washed outcroppings and small islands that form the shoreline, reaching open waters beyond the sheltered bay. The scene, still more than half an hour's ride in the distance, spreads out in front of him. Navy anti-submarine aircraft buzz the site, dropping flares attached to parachutes. The lights glide down too gently and illuminate the fog with an unsettling orange glow. The air is charged with jet fuel and its overwhelming stench.

Many other vessels are scattered on the water, including a Canadian Navy supply ship. Commander Rick Town of *HMCS Preserver* had been told that a passenger plane lost contact and possibly crashed at sea. The *Preserver* was conducting exercises near the search area, and Commander Town was immediately dispatched to give aid. It took little time to find the expanse of floating wreckage approximately five nautical miles southwest of Peggy's Cove.

The *Preserver* sits anchored at the edge of the debris field. She serves as instant morgue and on-scene command center for the rescue and recovery, dubbed "Operation Persistence." Commander

Town directs the fleet of volunteer helpers on the water. Fishermen, Bob included, use channel six on the VHF. Town gives grid coordinates for each boat to search. The sound of his reassuringly calm and considered voice soothes the fishermen searching for survivors. Someone is in charge.

The debris field is vast and thick with detritus, but it's dark and the forms are difficult to discern. Boats idle, bright dots in a wavering expanse of blackness, and shine their spotlights over their assigned grids, trying to find human shapes in the mess. Bob sees a doll. This is the closest thing he's seen to a human shape, so he manoeuvres around and hangs out far over the railing to pull the sopping bundle onboard. He lifts it up in front of him with his hands around its waist. The lights from the flares illuminate the figure and Bob realizes he's holding a human infant. Parts of the child are missing but there is no blood. Bob feels calm and full of faith.

An overwhelming need to properly care for the body of this victim comes over him and time slows. Gratitude flushes away any sense of horror. Bob was chosen; woken from slumber, driven to his boat, and pulled out to sea alone to care for this little body. He treats the child's remains with reverence, wrapping it in a blanket and laying it gently beside him, then signals with his spotlight that he's found something of importance.

The rain picks up as Bob hands his small charge over the boat rail and into the arms of another volunteer who will ferry the remains to the *Preserver* and, eventually, into the hands of Dr. Butt and his team.

* * *

David and Janet Wilkins arrive at the home of friends in Maple Valley, Washington, around the time Robert Conrad is heading out to sea on the east coast. The television news is reporting a Swissair plane down off the coast of Halifax. David and Janet realize it's their son's plane; it's Monte's plane. CNN is reporting survivors. There is an 800 number flashing across the bottom of the screen. David calls, but the person on the other end can only confirm that the plane has crashed and nothing else.

"If you leave your name and number, we'll get back to you."

* * *

"We want to offer our help. We'll get you as many body bags as you need, as soon as we can," a supplier from Atlanta tells John. It's not more than two hours since the plane disappeared and already the information has travelled through the international media to the southern States and back to John at his office.

"Well, that is very generous of you. Very generous. But I'm afraid it would be impossible for me to accept them as such. Everything will have to be processed through appropriate channels, you see." John wishes he could say yes. Getting anything extra out of this Nova Scotia government is like pulling teeth. He hates his dinky, grimy office on the first floor, right by the front door. He hates it almost as much as the small-minded bureaucracy he finds pervasive in his new home province.

With everything packed to go, and no destination in mind, it's time to search for marching orders. John calls his boss, Deputy Minister Gordon Gillis. Gordon's son answers the phone.

* * *

"Dad, there's this guy on the phone whose name is Butt. He needs to talk to the Deputy Attorney General or something, and he says it's urgent. Do you think it might be a prank?"

Gordon forces himself awake and takes the phone. "What's the problem, John?"

Gordon met John before he became Nova Scotia's Chief ME. The Nova Scotia Government had been dealing with a grieving family who would not accept the local police or medical expert's interpretation of their son's death. They insisted he was killed in police custody.

In the fall of 1993, Gordon Gillis, then new to the role of Deputy Minister, inherited this political hot potato from his predecessor. He consulted Wayne Cochrane, a Department of Justice lawyer who knew Dr. Butt by reputation. John was one of the few British-trained forensic experts in the field, and he was considered one of the best. He didn't come cheap, but Gordon felt the high-profile case needed a high-profile specialist.

Five years after his death, with the public battle still raging, the deceased boy's parents had given consent to have their son's body exhumed. John had performed a thorough exam of the corpse and made extensive notes, which Gordon read. He couldn't imagine how John dealt with the horror described in those pages. The corpse was badly decomposed and barely recognizable after years in a watery grave. Gordon thought John did a terrific job. He was tough, aggressive, and called it as he saw it. He was the perfect guy for the case.

A few years after the inquest, Nova Scotia was in the market for a new Chief Medical Examiner. Once again, Gordon found himself thinking of Dr. Butt.

"We'll never get him," Gordon told his boss. "He's too expensive, and he won't come here. We don't have the resources."

But Gordon knew there weren't many qualified people to choose from and John was at the top of that short list, so he offered him the position, despite his belief that John would turn it down. To his great surprise, John accepted. That was almost three years ago.

John's voice sounds tight over the phone, "I suppose you haven't heard yet. A big passenger plane went down somewhere off the Aspotogan Peninsula. Linda and I are at the office and we've packed up. We're ready to move now."

Gordon shakes the sleep from his mind. This is not a prank call. The wheels are spinning. He has to brush away the sleep and think fast. "Go to the RCMP headquarters," he says. Everyone, everywhere, must be scrambling.

After Gordon sends John off, he calls the RCMP Assistant Commissioner, Dwight Bishop.

"What is the status?" Gordon asks.

"Major airline incident up the coast. Looks really bad. We have command set up. It's going to be bad."

"Listen, I hate to ask you this at a time like this, but I need a favour."

"Whatever you need," Bishop says.

"Can you adopt John? Do what has to be done to help him out? We don't have the admin help they're going to need. I know you guys have to shift major priorities, but can you shift one more and adopt him?"

Without a second of hesitation, Bishop responds, "Done." The chain of command is everything to the RCMP.

* * *

Between the ME's office and the RCMP headquarters, there are four cemeteries in the midst of downtown Halifax. The graves dug into the hillside above the harbour occupy prime real estate. Weathered grey headstones pocked with green and black lichen overlook the inlet vista. Their engravings, if still discernible, show dates as far back as 1749 when the British settlement was first named the *Town of Halifax* after an English earl. Graveyards populate the coastline beyond the city as well. White-clad Anglican churches with steep roofs and surrounding gravestones cling to the rocks along the shoulders of winding rural roads. The hardy people here are no strangers to tragedy.

On April 14, 1912, the *Titanic* went down in the Atlantic Ocean. Ships from Halifax were sent to recover the drowned in the days following the luxury cruise ship's demise. Hundreds of bodies were pulled from the icy water. Some of them rest in these cemeteries.

By far the biggest maritime disaster on this coast took place on December 6, 1917 when two ships collided in the Halifax Harbour. One of the vessels, the *Mont-Blanc*, was laden with explosives. The collision caused a fire, which attracted the attention of the people going about their business on the busy downtown hillside. Twenty minutes after the initial incident, with a crowd of spectators gathered round, the *Mont-Blanc* exploded and killed nearly two thousand people in a split second. Then, too, the people of Halifax sprang to action, everyone alive helping in any way possible.

John and Linda head to the RCMP building, passing the gravestone markers in the cemeteries filled with other disaster victims. Steve Duncan, the RCMP Chief Superintendent, Dwight Bishop, and McCloskey are waiting for them. Thursday is only a few hours old.

They hold a planning meeting in a room where boxes and stacks of papers line the walls. John feels uneasy. He doesn't think Chief Superintendent Duncan has a clue. John doesn't have a clear plan either, but at the very least, he has disaster experience. They discuss the morgue. Duncan wants to talk about communications. How will the chain of evidence work within the morgue? How will they catalogue the material? Where will the evidence be kept?

John doesn't like the direction this is going. He's more concerned with finding the right place, and right now. The morgue is his territory, and the remains are his until he releases them. It's the usual bulldozing behaviour from these cops. Thankfully, McCloskey and Bishop are present, ensuring the ME's concerns are addressed.

John and Linda climb back into his bronze Jeep Cherokee and follow McCloskey to the Emergency Measures Office (EMO) on Water Street, across from the pier, down the hill from the cemeteries. The meeting at the EMO is about finding John whatever he needs, and a location that can handle the scope of the work: lots of space, a secure perimeter, access to offices. The space must allow for makeshift morgues, running water, good lighting, efficient drainage, and privacy. The lot must be big enough for helicopters and naval planes to land and take off. It needs to be on the waterfront, somewhere large vessels can access. The Emergency Measures Officer is nodding, making notes. Things are feeling a bit better, a bit more organized. John thinks this man must have a military background.

"Anything else?" the EM officer asks.

"Refrigeration. A good deal of refrigeration," John replies. "We'll need to hire refrigerated trucks, so there'll have to be space for them to park right next to the morgue set-up."

"How many trucks are we talking here?"

John does a rough calculation in his head, still knowing practically nothing about the number of victims or how long it will take to do the job. He feels a bit of panic. This is all going to cost a lot of money. Right now, right here, with his list of needs, he will blow his annual budget. *How many trucks?*

"Four or five, I should think." John is apprehensive, but what can be done about it? This is the job, and all expense aside, it must be done.

The Canadian Forces Base Shearwater in Dartmouth, across the bridge from Halifax, is chosen as the best location. Two airplane hangars sit side by side. In Hangar A, the Transportation Safety Board will rebuild the downed plane from the recovered wreckage. John's team will examine and identify human remains in Hangar B.

Not long before sunrise on Thursday, September 3rd, John, Linda, and Pat McCloskey arrive at Hangar B on the Shearwater base. The space is cavernous and empty, despite the few offices around the perimeter. Solid concrete floors and soaring ceilings with distant florescent lights are immediately disconcerting. There are no sinks in sight, no obvious drainage holes in the cement, no power plugs, except a few in each office. There is, however, a grid of bright yellow tape marking 300 grave-sized rectangles covering the concrete floor.

Chapter Five

PATHOLOGY

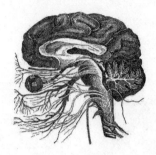

THE DISMISSAL LETTER came in March. After his mother's death, John had moved numbly through his fourth and supposedly final year of medical school. He felt the pull of the Navy keenly, and it kept him from his studies on many occasions. By the spring, he was back in trouble with the university. John's absences from surgery, one of the only departments that kept track, were too many. He was barred from writing his final exams. If he wanted to be a doctor, to fulfill Isobel's vision for his life, he'd have to start fourth year all over again.

Part of him felt relief. *Was he really meant to be a doctor, or was it all her idea?* His thoughts inched closer to an officer's life. Medical school continued to be an uphill battle. He'd failed his entire first year because that prissy Professor Tuba gave him 48% on the biochemistry final. If you failed anything in first year med, you had to do the entire year over. His buddies, and all the ones who had come up with him from pre-med, went on without him.

After two tries at first year medicine, John moved up to second year, hoping he'd put the worst of it behind him. Then he failed the pathology final exam. Fortunately, students didn't get booted from second year for failing one class. Now, finally in his last year, he'd been kicked out again. Esteem, for John, was proving hard to come by at medical school.

Contrary to his life at university, every summer in the Navy pushed him up the ladder of success. The thought of starting fourth year medicine all over made life at sea look like a brilliant future, but the wave of Navy daydreams didn't wash down the wad of guilt stuck in his throat. He had to tell his father. *Be practical*, he told himself. *Get control of yourself.*

If he was to finish, next fall presented the first opportunity, and that was five months away. The Navy might give him paid work in the meantime. Going to sea removed him, at least temporarily, from duty as the good son. The opportunity to tell his father that he'd failed at medical school again came shortly after he received notice from the Navy that they had a post for him as an officer on a mine sweeper.

John met his dad and a few of Jack's salesmen colleagues in the dining room at Hotel Macdonald, a stately limestone chateau with copper dormers overlooking the North Saskatchewan River in downtown Edmonton. The dining room, laid with white cloth and silver, was a colony of businessmen making deals over a roast-beef luncheon. John suffered through his meal, dreading what was coming.

"I'm sorry to interrupt, but I need to speak with my dad about something."

"Well, my room is empty. Go on up there, if you like," Jack's boss said, handing over the key.

Father and son stood silent, shoulder-to-shoulder, on the elevator ride up a few floors to the new rectangular hotel addition. The original, castle-like hotel was built in 1915 when decadence was in high fashion. The new concrete wing, added in 1953, was defiantly incongruent next to the gracious peaks and curves of the limestone original. Modernism was having its way with design, and simplicity became the mark of wealth, but the shoebox addition was not popular with the locals.

John knew his father was a patient man. He wouldn't ask any questions or make any demands until John was ready to talk. He sensed no trepidation from his father, but his own heart was in his throat. The key slid into the lock easily, then the two men were alone, standing face to face. Jack was silent, waiting calmly. John pushed down his fear and started plainly.

"I have to tell you that I've been asked to leave medical school."

Jack looked struck. His voice quivered. "Why?"

"I've missed too many days in surgery." John was forcing his words, holding himself hostage until the whole truth was out. "My absences preclude me from writing the exams, so there is no reason to continue with the year."

Jack wept. It was unheard of, and the outpouring terrified John. He'd never seen his dad break down. It was like Jack was spilling all the tears John had stuffed down to be Isobel's son.

After the confession to his father, and Jack's unprecedented reaction, John knew he had to finish medical school. Jack needed it, and John needed to be the kind of man who did the right thing. Too many sacrifices had been made for his education. He would soldier on, despite the mounting list of medical-school failures. He would succeed, despite his desire to give up.

In the spring of 1960, six years after starting the four-year program, John graduated from the University of Alberta as a General Practitioner of Medicine. Dreams of a military career lingered still and he hoped to find a medical post somewhere in the Navy. It was his compromise. He'd satisfied his duty as a son and felt free to pursue a life at sea.

After graduation, young Dr. Butt took a position as a clinic physician for the summer season at the Banff Springs Hotel. The towering, hewn-stone chateau, built in the 1880s, was considered a holiday jewel in the Rocky Mountain crown. The steep rock range rises up on Alberta's southwestern border in stark contrast to the heartland of gently rolling hills. The mountains form a natural barrier between the conservative cattlemen of the plains and the tree-loving hippies on the west coast. Fences and neighbours come to mind.

One morning at the posh hotel, a Catholic priest from New Jersey had a stroke at the door of his room. While Dr. Butt knelt on the floor attending to the priest, a hotel patron passed by and, stepping over the protruding feet of the unconscious patient, muttered, "Oh, excuse me, Father."

Dr. Butt had to stifle a snicker. *As if the priest will take offense!* People were so silly.

A small plane flew into Banff, low on fuel and light enough to land and take off in the tight mountain valley. John was sent to accompany the man of God to Newark, New Jersey with a nurse. The priest, in his semi-conscious haze, pulled repeatedly at his catheter. The nurse, on her way to becoming a nun in the Catholic order, was too demure to handle the patient's genitals. John was not impressed with her helplessness in the situation.

Earlier in the summer, John had read two collections of medical stories: *Eleven Blue Men*, a compilation of true death mysteries and the sleuthing doctors who solve them; and *Bellevue is My Home*, stories about life in the New York City charity hospital, written by Salvatore Cutolo, the Deputy Medical Administrator of Bellevue Hospital at the time. After John finished his duties in New Jersey, he spent a few days in New York City. He decided to investigate the famous hospital. There, a gregarious Salvatore Cutolo, busy with payday duties, sent the young doctor off on his own, saying, "Go wherever you like."

Bellevue, a sprawling red brick building of the Victorian era, had strong roots in pathology. In 1854, Dr. James Wood, a surgeon at the hospital, fathered a bill, passed by the US Congress, making dissection of cadavers legal in New York State. Systematic autopsies started that same year, and in 1866, the first New York City morgue was established at the hospital.

John found the ER frantically busy, as all indigent medical cases from the streets of NYC passed through its doors. He introduced himself to the staff when the moments allowed and wished he had a white lab coat so he at least looked like a doctor. He observed a few intakes, and discussed the details of a case. A young girl had been found comatose from a drug overdose. Her still body made a small, crumpled heap on the slender ER cot. He felt like an intruder, looking down at the lost girl in her vulnerable state. He had no business there, gawking at her. *That's it*, he thought, *I'm done with this tour*, and headed outside to reassess his visit.

John walked around the grounds of the hospital, taking in the complicated series of wings and courtyards, and chanced upon the back entrance to the morgue. Through the door and into a garage, large vans were parked next to a stack of rough wooden coffins. Two men loaded the crates into the vans. John ventured in to query the workers. The crude boxes contained the bodies of unclaimed, unnamed homeless headed to a pauper's graveyard. Again, John was overcome with the feeling that his presence was an intrusion. People deserved dignity, even in death. Though he was curious about the workings of the morgue, propriety got the better of him, and he gave up on his self-guided investigation.

After three months in Banff, John found a medical position with the Navy. In April of 1962, he was at sea serving as the medical officer for a squadron of four escort vessels. He traversed from vessel to vessel on a jackstay. The ships lined up side-by-side, travelling at the same clip, and two lines were rigged over the water between them. On a small seat, perched several stories above the churning water, the doctor was pulled from one vessel to the other like laundry on a clothesline. By this point in his Navy career, a ride in the jackstay was old news—one more way to be a fearless man in uniform.

After a young petty officer had a scuffle with one of his mates, life at sea became a little more frightening. The incident was, no doubt, fueled by alcohol and the resulting suspension of inhibitions. According to those present, the petty officer made an overtly sexual pass at another man and received a black eye, detainment, and possible court-martialing for expressing his desire. The sick bay was the only place to house the offender while the squadron sailed on, and it made John terribly uncomfortable to share his domain with the accused.

During John's first year as a cadet at sea back in the fifties, some of the young cadets had returned from shore leave with stories about a high-ranking officer and sexual innuendos. "Commander Crilly fruited one of the guys!" they said. The rumour spread within hours.

After that, Lieutenant Commander Crilly was nowhere to be found on the base, and John never saw him again. It was his first example of how the wrong kind of men were treated by the military. John had been further informed on the wrong kind of men while attending medical school when a psychiatrist lectured on sexual psychopaths. The visiting professor stated unequivocally that men having sex with men was dangerous behaviour. In the Navy, "sexual deviants" were expelled or court-martialed. Men with secrets were considered a soft spot in the wall of defence, and lust-filled men were weak links in the chain of command.

On rounds of the ship, Dr. Butt did his best to avoid the petty officer who had shown his true colours, but the sick bay was a necessary stop on his rounds. Seeing the defeated man hiding in a bottom bunk with his swollen eye made John feel ill. He thought of his own self-control. He thought of Alex, his boyhood friend, and how they carried on, and how good it felt. What if he slipped? What if he had too much to drink? It wasn't uncommon to get drunk in the Navy, that was certain. John was terrified of possible shame. If any fellow made a pass, he'd beat him to a pulp.

The bridge, command, and the uniform all continued to hold allure despite the risk. But John's tolerance for the hierarchy of military life ended one morning on the bridge of a fleet ship. He enjoyed his habit of watching the activity and chatting with the officers every morning. Captain E.T.G. Madgwick, a war veteran who had guided successful rescue missions in the Bermuda Triangle and survived a ship's mutiny as First Lieutenant, popped on the bridge for his morning inspection. John didn't pay much attention.

"Doctor, don't you salute your commanding officer in the morning?" the Captain asked in his puckish, English accent.

John brought a stiff hand to his brow and thought, *That's it, I can't handle this crap anymore!* The insistent chain of command, the excessive drinking, the hiding, and the fear collapsed his childhood dream. He'd endured many things to wear the uniform, but the constant hierarchical ass kissing was beyond what his ego could bear. He left the Navy for good in the spring of 1962.

He moved on to family practice with a position in Comox, a small port town on the east coast of Vancouver Island in British Columbia with a population of barely two thousand people. The middle-aged doctor who hired John had a family and was ready to let a younger man take over the on-call hours of his practice. It was still common at the time to call the family doctor in the middle of the night if a child was running a high fever, or someone felt ill, or even if a mother-to-be wasn't sure the pains were real labour or simply a pre-labour visit from Braxton Hicks.

John settled in and adopted a basset hound he named George. When those three-in-the-morning calls happened, the young doctor jumped out of bed, nerves jangling. He'd assess the situation and head out to soothe a sore throat or stop a bad bout of diarrhea. There was no point in not going. He'd lie awake worrying over it anyway, so might as well go and be sure. "C'mon, George. C'mon!" he'd say to the dog. But George remained resolutely camped at the end of the warm bed and gave a warning growl if poked.

The senior doctor made his junior feel less than appreciated. A pregnant woman had developed complications so John had her admitted to hospital. When the older doctor returned and walked the first rounds with John, they spent a few minutes with the mother to be. The senior doc patted her hand and smiled benevolently. Addressing John, while keeping his gazed fixed on the patient, he said, "Well, she'll feel better now that I'm back, won't she?"

Why get up in the middle of the night while George snores away just to be dismissed like that in front of a patient? Why get up in the middle of the night at all? Family practice wasn't the right fit. And the small town felt suffocating—everybody in everybody else's business.

By the fall of 1963, John was back on the mainland, and in the metropolis, working and studying at Vancouver General Hospital (VGH) as an open-ended resident under the umbrella of the University of British Columbia. He chose to study internal medicine with a special interest in neurology. Autopsy work was a necessary component at the time.

John was uneasy with dissection at first. Personhood clung to the remains. He covered the faces of the cadavers with a white cloth before making the Y incision. He tried to distance himself from the idea that he was pulling someone apart, someone who had a life and possibly a family. Eventually, after many autopsies, he became accustomed to the process. Once the body was open, he removed the breastbone and ribs covering the heart and lungs, then tied off the intestine and removed the small bowel to keep it from flopping around while he worked. Very carefully, so as not to buttonhole the skin of the face with his scalpel, he cut the tongue away from under the jaw and pulled it down through the neck, then slid his scalpel along the backbone through the soft connective tissue, freeing the collection of organs and tubes from the body cavity. This allowed him to pull out the organs en masse.

The brain was more difficult. The face was unavoidable for at least the first few minutes. He sliced the scalp from behind one ear, over the top of the head, to the matching mastoid process on the other side, then pulled the front scalp down over the face, exposing the skull. A saw was used to cut through the calvarium, a thick bone skullcap protecting the brain, and expose the dura mater membrane. When the gray matter was accessible, a cut was made at the top of the spinal column and the final vital organ removed.

The mechanisms of human internal operation were then laid out for examination. Weights and measurements, samples for histology and toxicology, and any manner of test or examination were taken or performed as needed. When the investigation was complete, all of the removed parts were placed in a stout and sturdy plastic bag and returned to the body cavity before the Y incision was stitched shut.

Autopsies at VGH were performed largely to study cases of chronic disease. The results contributed to compilations of data sets. There was nothing to solve in the moment, the mysteries of why and how already over. That is, until a patient in John's ward died of an unknown cause. The man had been incarcerated at the Oakalla Prison Farm in the city Burnaby, a suburb of metro Vancouver. At some point in the night, the prisoner rolled off the top bunk and was found face down, deeply unconscious on the concrete floor the following morning. Officials rushed the prisoner to Vancouver General but he died before the doctors were able to diagnose his disease. The Coroner ordered an official autopsy, per provincial law, and the body was taken downtown to the Vancouver morgue at the corner of Cordova and Main.

At the autopsy, there was an immediate mystery pertaining to the body on the table. What was the manner and cause of this man's death? The deceased was in custody when he died. Was his demise facilitated by this fact? John had to know how things turned out, so he thought to attend the autopsy. Eventually, after the lab tests were processed, tuberculosis meningitis was found. Mystery, John discovered, made autopsy work meaningful. The bodies on the tables at medical-legal autopsies kept their identities out of necessity and provided an end for the means of their mutilated remains. Forensic pathology was intriguing, but John believed neurology was the specialty for him.

By his second year at VGH, John was the president of the residents association. He'd started dating a pretty nursing student named Barb. Life as a doctor was finally working out. Barb and John had mutual friends and enjoyed socializing together. She was slender and pleasant with long, golden hair—the opposite of hot-blooded Nora, his last girlfriend. Nora was a petite, raven-haired minx and he'd enjoyed her ravenous sexual appetite. They'd even done it on the living room floor at the family home while his dad slept upstairs.

But he liked Barb, despite her more demure attitude. They had fun together.

In the spring of 1964, when John proposed to Barb, marriage was still easy to get into, but hard to dissolve. Divorce was a word only whispered. Successful men—men with power and prestige—were married men with families, not bachelors with questionable social lives. Since John felt he was on his way with his residency at Vancouver General Hospital, it was time to conquer the next challenge on the road to success.

In the fall of 1964, John and Barb were married at St. Philip's Anglican Church on the west side of Vancouver in the wealthy

Dunbar neighbourhood. The church was modest in size, with a soaring vaulted ceiling of dark wood rafters, whitewashed walls, and wooden pews. Arched windows with stained glass panels depicting biblical scenes made the most of the room's height, creating a sense of space in the small church. The late October sun shone through the stained glass scenes and illuminated the walls with coloured shadows of Christ, saints, and sacrificial lambs. John dressed in a white dinner jacket, black bow tie, and black tuxedo trousers. Barb wore a white dress. The reception dinner at the Vancouver Lawn, Tennis & Badminton Club was a posh affair. According to custom, Barb's father footed the bill.

John's career prospects were looking bright. He'd already sent feelers out for positions in neurology and was offered a short-term residency at a prestigious hospital in London. He relished the thought of working in the UK, if briefly, at the famous National Hospital for Nervous Disorders in Queen's Square. Since he wasn't due to start the new position until the fall of 1965, the newlyweds set up house in Vancouver to ride out the winter.

Once they were married, their already reserved love life suffered from the pressure of forever. John's affection for his wife quickly wore thin. During that first winter together in Vancouver, Barb became ill with a dangerously high fever. For several days, John sat on the couch watching television in the evenings while she suffered alone in bed. He knew his lack of compassion was telling, but he ignored the signs of indifference. He wanted to be a successful doctor with a well-educated wife and promising, dutiful offspring. Nothing else would satisfy, and some romantic idea of love wasn't going to spoil the picture. They just needed time to build their life together. The care, he hoped, would come with the passing years. But a little voice in his head, barely audible from years of suffocation, strongly disagreed with this marriage.

A three-week spring voyage to the United Kingdom temporarily rejuvenated John and Barb's strained relationship. They sailed on the Oriana, an enormous and perfectly appointed vessel in the Orient Steam Navigation Company fleet. Fine dining in the Elizabethan

Restaurant, cocktails in the Carnival Room, dancing the night away in the Ocean Bar and Disco, lounging by the Dragon Pool on the Verandah deck, and walking the endless open and covered promenades kept the newlyweds blissfully busy in the lap of seafaring luxury. John was in his element at sea and enjoyed the ship immensely.

In London, they quickly found a flat in Regent's Park and John started his residency at the hospital in Queen's Square. He didn't plan on building a long-term life in England, but heading back to Canada with this hospital on his resume was bound to open doors. The London shine didn't last long. Working at Vancouver General had been easy compared to this new hospital in a new country. He had no connections or influence and insecurity bubbled up after a conversation with one of the older doctors.

"Where are you from, Dr. Butt?"

"I'm Canadian."

"Ah, I see," the British doctor said. "I've visited Montreal and I discovered something while I was there."

"What's that?" John asked, expecting something about the weather.

"Canadians are lazy."

John didn't take the time to point out the diversity of his expansive home country. He consoled himself in the moment by blaming the French. Albertans and Quebecois carry the Canadian torch in the English versus French rivalry. But the slight was enough to have him contemplating a hasty return to Canada.

The marriage, too, felt more and more like a mistake. The young doctor found a grotty little pub on the edge of Regent's Park near Camden Town, walking distance from the flat he shared with his young wife, an ocean away from their friends and family. The pub's dark interior, heavy with wood, exuded a gloom that matched John's rankled demeanour. Six months after the start of his new life in Great Britain, he sat drinking bitters and having a conversation with himself. *Okay, that's a good boy. You're doing fine, now. You just keep at it.* He knew his marriage was doomed but he wanted to shove that aside. Women were fine. He'd already accepted life as a husband and he wanted a family. Barb, in John's opinion, was making it tough.

They hardly had enough of a sex life for John, and it seemed to him she was increasingly taking to her bed without him.

One morning, near the end of his contract with the National Hospital for Nervous Diseases, John stood before a poster advertising a lecture by Dr. Francis Camps at the London Hospital of Forensic Pathology. Camps, a soft-featured, smiling man with a Sherlock-style smoking pipe, had pioneered methods in forensic medicine and garnered fame working with the police. John was intrigued, and the lecture proved quite fascinating. His contract with the National Hospital was coming to an end and he needed a new job, but he knew his chances for advancement in the UK were slim. The only way to promotion was to fill dead men's shoes, and he wasn't waiting around for that. He knew it was time to go home, but thought he might as well investigate forensic pathology a bit more before they left.

To make ends meet, John administered immigration physicals for the Canadian High Commission in London. Barb found a job at a fancy store on Regent Street and started building a social circle of her own. John took to asking around about opportunities to study and work in forensic pathology. He and Barb had joined a few upper-crust networking groups. Professional contacts were to be cultivated and John was proving a brilliant collector of useful connections. Through his acquaintance at the Canadian High Commission, he landed an interview with Professor Keith Simpson at Guy's Hospital in London. Simpson, a slender, stern-looking fellow with a considerate disposition, was the first professor of forensic medicine at Guy's and had written a textbook on the subject. He was also an adversary of Professor Camps. Both were considered leading experts at the time, and the prestige made them competitive.

At the interview, John sat across from Simpson, ready to make his best impression. "Thank you for meeting with me, Professor."

The senior doctor perused John's resume. "I have to tell you from the start, you don't have enough training in pathology to work in the field. You'll have to go back to the very beginning."

"Well, I'm interested in learning more." John didn't feel slighted by the doctor's assessment. It was true.

"You can shadow me for a few months and observe all of my cases. But you won't be able to participate in the work, and you won't get paid."

"That sounds fine." Since he had paid work with the High Commission whenever he wanted it, and Barb was also working, there was enough time and money to accept the austere offer.

"Alright, Dr. Butt, let's see what kind of aptitude you have for this sort of thing."

After that, John travelled from one mortuary to the next and the next as an unpaid observer. Though he wasn't getting hands-on experience, the professor did a great deal of teaching and questioning while he worked. It didn't take long for John to be sure—the mix of medicine, mystery, and justice enthralled him. No more treating live patients. His future was with the dead.

CHAPTER SIX

PRESERVER

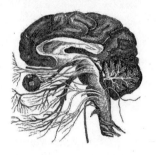

10:14 p.m., Wednesday, September 2nd, 1998

"SWISSAIR ONE ELEVEN heavy is declaring Pan Pan Pan. We have smoke in the cockpit . . ."

Flight 111, travelling from New York City to Geneva, departed from the John F. Kennedy airport at 8:18 p.m. that evening. No problems had been communicated to control before the first alarm concerning smoke. The triple-pan code signifies urgent trouble, though not emergency. The Moncton High Level Controller in New Brunswick, the center conducting high-altitude air traffic on the eastern coast of Canada, suggests the plane land in Halifax.

Communication with Swissair 111 passes to the Halifax Terminal Controller. "Swissair one eleven, when you have time, could I have the number of souls on board and your fuel onboard please, for emergency services?"

"Roger, at the time the fuel is two zero three tonnes. We must dump some fuel. May we do that in this area during descent?"

The plane, at this point in its trajectory, is loaded with fuel. Landing a wide-bodied—or heavy—jet full of fuel requires a longer airstrip than Halifax has to offer.

"Swissair one-eleven roger, turn to the left heading of two zero

zero degrees and advise me when you are ready to dump. It will be about ten miles before you are off the coast. You are still within about twenty-five miles of the airport."

Ten minutes after the triple-pan signal, the autopilot-disconnect alarm sounds in the cockpit.

"At the time, we must fly manually ..."

The pilot and co-pilot are audibly stressed while attempting to turn, descend, and dump their fuel load with limited power.

"Swissair one eleven heavy is declaring emergency."

"Swissair one eleven, just a couple of miles. I'll be right with you," control responds.

"And we are declaring emergency now Swissair one eleven ..." These are the last words to Halifax Control at 10:25 p.m., approximately eleven minutes after the first distress call. The recorded altitude of the vessel is 9700 feet, just shy of 3000 metres.

At 10:31 p.m., after six minutes of radio silence, Swissair 111 slams into the water, nose first and nearly upside down, at approximately 550 kilometres per hour.

* * *

Major Crimes Constable Rick Chadwick is a young and promising RCMP officer with a push-broom moustache, dark hair worn slick, and an imposing stature. Only a few hours ago, Rick had been cozy in bed next to his beautiful wife. Now he's on a whaling boat in the dark, traversing the choppy water of St. Margaret's Bay.

Like so many others, Rick had been roused from his slumber by a ringing phone.

"We got a plane crash out in Peggy's Cove area. St. Margaret's Bay. Looks like it's going to be a big investigation so we need Major Crimes. Grab your stuff and head over to the Tantallon detachment." Rick's commander was brief, and had little in the way of details.

"Little plane or big plane?" Rick had asked, trying to shake the sleep inertia.

"I don't know."

Must be a Cessna, Rick thought. He, too, mentally denied the possibility of a large-scale tragedy and left home with a small crash bag thinking he'd be back in a day or two.

Constable Chadwick listened to the police scanner while he drove to the station. *Why are they talking about boats?* Within an hour of his arrival at the Tantallon Detachment near the top of the bay, Rick received his assignment to Exhibit Collections on *HMCS Preserver,* the Navy ship serving as command center at the disaster scene.

From the whaling boat, the scene on the water looks like the front line of a floating war zone. It is a rollercoaster ride through a house of horrors. Sea King helicopters fly low over the water, shining spotlights on the floating mess. C130 aircraft swoop back and forth across the mile-wide debris field. The horizon is a moving target.

When the whaling boat is close enough to its destination, a small Zodiac pulls alongside and two Navy personnel wave the RCMP officers aboard. Rick feels like a Keystone Cop. Seven men in a tiny dinghy, hanging over the sides, covered in sea-spray and wobbling over the waves. When the dinghy reaches the hull of the *Preserver,* a rope ladder is sent down. The roiling water moves the lumbering Navy ship, rocking it starboard to port like a giant's cradle. The ladder dips and rises, close to the Zodiac, then 15 feet up as the huge ship rolls in the swell. The Navy men use the small craft's outboard motor to manoeuvre the dinghy close to the wall of metal.

One of the seamen hollers over the ocean's roar. "When the ship rolls toward us, grab the ladder, put your feet solidly on the rung, and hang on, because you're going to go up!"

A soaking wet Chadwick takes his turn without incident, as do his mates, but things don't get better from there. The RCMP officers split in two groups to sort debris brought from the smaller boats on the water. They separate the human remains from the personal effects. Things like purses, passports, and footwear go to one group. The human material comes to Chadwick's group in the refrigeration hold on the ship.

Body bags from local fishing boats litter the floor of the cold

and cavernous metal room. Chadwick knows his job, and he is all
business. No time for emotional reactions now. The most important
thing is the chain of evidence. He is the protector of proof. If this
disaster is someone's fault, or worse, someone's intention, everything
he touches could convict a mass murderer.

* * *

At the crash site, sometime before dawn, Bob Conrad has a sad
epiphany. There are no survivors to rescue. The destruction is complete. He turns back to make the one-hour journey to the dock and
then home. During the ride, his state of mind takes a drastic turn.
The calmness he felt when caring for the child's body is gone. In its
place he feels overwhelming sadness. Drizzling rain turns to a down-
pour, punctuating the discomfort. The horror of the scene floods
over him. The enormity of this disaster and what it will mean for his
community and his livelihood is overtaking the grace he had cultivated in the moment of service.

In the early morning, Bob arrives back at the door to his warm
home. He steps into the short entrance hall that leads to the open
kitchen and living room, to the large wooden table where his family
gathers, and to the sliding glass doors that frame a picturesque view
of the sea. He wonders if the bay will ever be the same. Somewhere
out on the water, the old version of Bob was pulled overboard. He
sees with new eyes, his minds reels with new memories, and he feels
too much.

The Conrad's phone rings incessantly. Reporters from Canada,
the States, and Europe are hungry for information and they have no
regard for the hour or privacy. They call everyone they can find who
lives close to the crash site. Bob was out on the water, and has seen
what they want to hear. Politely, patiently, numbly, he turns them
away. His time with the child was sacred and he will not disrespect
the job he was given by sensationalizing his experience.

* * *

John takes the boardroom in Hangar B at Shearwater for his office. His time is split between giving directions and talking on the phone. All the while, he monitors his internal state. The physical responses to stress can empower action, to a point. His heart continues to race and he feels a great sense of unease, but keeps it contained below the surface of outward operations. The mental lists he compiles are keeping his mind from frying in an adrenaline overload.

The most important job at hand is to identify everyone who was on the plane. According to the flight manifest they received from Swissair, there were 215 passengers and 14 crewmembers—229 people in total. John's team will also need to note the injuries. Are there signs of fire, or patterns of similarity in broken bones? Any signs of injury from shrapnel?

Methods for identifying human remains have taken giant steps forward over the course of John's career. Beyond visual identification, fingerprint analysis has been in play the longest, with early examples dating back to the late 1800s. In 1984, a British geneticist discovered the key to identification by DNA analysis, providing the most succinct evidence of identity to date. But in cases of mass fatality, dental analysis often provides the best means of identification. Teeth are more durable than skin and dental x-rays are more efficient than DNA lab tests.

Each of the methods requires different tools, and John knows he may employ them all before his job is done. He has no time to think beyond the moment. The military and government offices on all levels call to ask what needs to be done. He requests a team of forensic dentists, and asks to borrow forensic specialists from the surrounding hospitals and provinces. John is a hub. He strives to create a system of spokes that support a giant wheel capable of carrying them all to the end of this nightmare.

The sun rises a little after six in the morning. John, Linda, and the team of workers hardly notice the day break, but they feel the march of time and the impending arrival of the dead. Elsewhere, the light signals a new stage for the rescue and recovery effort. Military personnel and volunteers begin walking the shorelines of the bay and all the small islands in the vicinity. With the dawn comes a short break in the weather. Those still out on the water are exposed to the first stark images of the crash site that display too clearly how violent the impact had been. Everyone who sees the disaster site loses hope.

Around 7 am, the doctor from *HMCS Preserver* radios in with a request for Dr. Butt. "I don't know where to start with all of this. I don't know where to begin," the doctor tells John. "Can you give me a hand and tell us what we should be doing?"

"I think I best come out there and see what you've got."

A Sea King helicopter transports John from the morgue-in-construction at Shearwater to the *Preserver*. Above the scene of destruction, he gets the first glimpse of debris. Small boats dot the surface with larger ships stationed at the edges of the scene. The entire area, a portion of sea that many fishermen call their workplace, is closed to all but those working on the recovery operation.

The ship's doctor shows John to the bridge where Commander Town is waiting. During the night, it was Commander Town who managed the fishermen, military personnel, and other helpers on the water. Rick Town was the beacon in the dark. After a night receiving one horror after another from the small vessels on the scene, Town might need a guiding light of his own. From the *Preserver's* bridge, John gets a closer look at the water. To the untrained eye, it's a largely unidentifiable mass of scattered debris, but John sees the human remains for what they are. Floating viscera mingles with hunks of caramel-coloured foam from the seat cushions, teddy bears, clothes, and luggage. Now he understands why they don't know how to deal with the situation. It's not as easy as putting bodies in bags and counting them off in whole numbers.

"Well, let's see what you've brought aboard and we'll figure it out from there," John tells the group of men as he scans the scene.

They lead him down to the bay where the remains are laid out. Pieces range from the smallest unrecognizable bits of flesh and bone, to torsos, some with a limb or two still attached. Most heads are severed at the jaw. There are hundreds of pieces. John suspects there will be thousands before they are done.

"We'll need to have some way of tracking each piece."

He can't possibly put an identity to every single bit of human remains. It would take years to repatriate each sliver to its owner and deliver their bodies to the grieving families. Continuity will be an issue. How far will his boss Gordon Gillis expect him to go? How small a piece? For now, he knows the job at hand. He must identify at least one piece of every person who was on that plane.

* * *

Ron Jeppesen, Supervisor of Construction Trade Services for Nova Scotia Public Works, arrives at his office a little later than usual on Thursday morning. He'd been reading the night before and forgot to set the alarm. It's 7:50 a.m. and the phone is already ringing.

"You have to get over to Shearwater right away. They're going to bring the bodies in and they need a morgue built."

"Excuse me? A morgue?" Ron hasn't turned on a television or a radio. He has no idea.

"Because of the plane crash. Go build them whatever they need."

On his way from the government building on Young street to Hangar B at Shearwater, Ron wonders what it will take to build a morgue. He's had ten years on the job and done a lot of things, but this one is new. He knows his team is solid. Whatever it takes, they'll get it done.

The grid of tape on the hangar's floor is the first thing that strikes Ron. The length of tape required to crisscross the vast floor insists on a moment of calculation for a man with a math-inclined mind. Linda is ready and eager with directions for him. She acts as the Medical Examiner's liaison with an extensive list of requirements. Ron listens carefully, only interrupting for occasional clarification. Then he gets on the phone and calls his team of trades superintendents: plumbers, electricians, carpenters, supply techs, even truckers.

Nova Scotia Public Works people hammer, saw, solder, and weld. They build a series of semi-closed rooms, quickly framed-in and covered with rough plywood. Some have a thin layer of clear plastic for a ceiling, but most are open to the cavernous expanse of the hangar overhead. The rooms are arranged like houses in a neighbourhood. A six-foot-wide back alley allows for the plumbing and electrical workings between back-to-back rows of the cubicles, with proper access through the hallways in front. Generators are set up outside the hangar, next to the plumbing chase filtration system. The sectioned-off spaces will be used for many things: change rooms, supply and file storage, dental x-ray stations, fingerprint stations, and several autopsy stations. Before long, the expansive cement floor is covered with a shantytown of plywood and plastic.

The second thing to strike Ron after his arrival at Shearwater is Dr. Butt himself. The man in charge of the morgue is wearing a florescent hard hat, topped with a tiny propeller, while racing around the hangar on an adult tricycle. Ron can't help but appreciate the efficiency of locomotion and identification, not to mention the relief of absurdity in the sombre proceedings.

* * *

The first human remains arrive at Shearwater by mid morning. Once the deliveries begin, the flow is constant. Helicopters shuffle the bags from the *Preserver* to the base in an endless loop. The sounds of rotor blades slicing the air approach and recede like an echo. Within twelve hours from John and Linda's arrival at the Shearwater Naval Base, the morgue is operational.

Linda listens to her boss's specific instructions on how specimens are to be received at the morgue. She thinks he's had the same conversation with the RCMP officers involved. Dr. Butt wants to know what is coming, when it is scheduled to arrive, how it will be delivered, and how it will be tagged. Linda herself has talked to the fellows at the RCMP to be sure they know the drill and are prepared to follow Dr. Butt's instructions.

After the first remains are processed, Linda gets a call from Inspector Lee Fraser, head of the RCMP's forensic identification unit in the Atlantic.

"Linda, what does Dr. Butt want to see me about?"

"I don't know." And she doesn't know, but she isn't surprised there is a problem already.

"Well I'm not going into any meeting with him unless you're there," Lee tells Linda.

In Dr. Butt's boardroom, Linda and several RCMP officers, including Inspector Fraser, are lectured on the systems once again.

Linda interrupts her boss. "Ok, well, we have to understand why you're upset. You already told us how you wanted everything."

"The RCMP are going ahead and doing whatever they want and I'm not in the know."

〜 "Alright, before we get into it,"—Linda talks like a mother— "you sat here and told me how you wanted this to go, and I went over it with the RCMP and they agreed to your system. So whatever happened this morning with the remains was exactly what you wanted to happen."

"But how do I know that they are following instructions? No one told me."

"I'll take the blame for that because I didn't let you know everything was happening the way you want it to. But since we all agreed, I thought it was a waste of time considering how busy we all are here."

"I always want to be kept in the loop." Dr. Butt is insistent.

"So I'll track you down and let you know that we're all following your instructions?" Linda thinks her question is obviously rhetorical.

"I need to know everything."

Essentially, that signals the end of the meeting. Linda leaves her boss's office wondering how much time she will spend in pointless meetings while this whole big thing is going on.

* * *

Communication is a big issue in a disaster. Residents in the area around St. Margaret's Bay are asked to keep phone use to a minimum because the circuits are overloaded. Reporters are calling everyone trying to get information. Family members call all of the official numbers they can find, searching for a shred of hope. Rescue workers, the Army, the Coast Guard, the Navy, and the RCMP are all calling back and forth, coordinating the needs of the recovery operation.

At the Shearwater morgue, one room is a dedicated communications center. They dub it the in-and-out center. There, RCMP members staff telephones, answering as many questions as possible, and taking in whatever information they can glean that may help identify passengers. John, for the most part, is shielded from the grieving family members, their onslaught of questions, and their tearful recitations of loved ones' belongings and identifying marks. But on the afternoon of this first operational day of the morgue, a stranger calls John on his private cell phone.

"Dr. Butt?"

"Yes."

"This is Rabbi Gluck. I'm calling from the medical examiner's office in New York. I am the Chaplain for the Port Authority Police here. I'm at the Office of the Medical Examiner. Dr. Hirsch sends his regards." The man on the other end has a distinct Yiddish accent.

"Yes, I see." John has no time for chat.

"I'm calling to ask that you not perform any autopsies on any of the Jewish passengers. Our faith does not condone these procedures and we don't want it done."

John is at a loss. How can he explain the situation to Rabbi Gluck?

"Well, it's still very early in the recovery process and we aren't entirely sure what we are dealing with here. All I can say now is that your request is noted and I will do what I can."

John ends the call abruptly and heads over to the communication room to warn the call centre about the Rabbi in case he should call them with demands. Ian, a young RCMP officer, is manning the desk. John likes Ian. He is very receptive, friendly, and easy to be around, unlike many of his superiors.

"You'll never guess what I've just been asked," John says to Ian. "I've had a rabbi call who doesn't want autopsies on the Jewish victims."

Ian pauses for a moment, then looks up from his phone. "Well, maybe you should just tell him to come up here and tell us which pieces are Jewish and we won't do autopsies on them."

John doesn't bother to stifle his guffaw. Humour, he has learned, is essential in times like these.

That night, approximately 24 hours after the crash, the first and only visually identifiable body arrives. It is the only body to momentarily occupy a space in the grid of tape on the floor of Hangar B.

CHAPTER SEVEN

HEROES

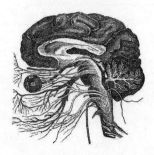

IN THE FALL of 1959, Steven Truscott, a fifteen-year-old boy, was sentenced to death by hanging. He'd been convicted of murder. The body of Lynne Harper, Truscott's classmate, had been found in the woods two days after she disappeared from the intersection of a country road and Highway Number Eight, near Clinton Air Force base in Ontario where they both lived. Lynne's blouse had been used as a ligature around her neck. The autopsy—carried out by Dr. John Penistan, a pathologist brought in from Stratford, and observed by David Hall Brooks, the local doctor—was performed under less-than-ideal conditions with little equipment. The analysis of stomach contents formed the crux of the prosecution's case. A very precise timeframe was determined by an inversely vague method. The pathologist used the state of Lynne Harper's last meal to determine a fifteen-minute window for her time of death. Dr. Penistan held a mason jar of translucent green stomach acid up to the light from a nearby window and gave it a shake. Hunks of semi-digested peas, carrots, and meat floated down and settled on the bottom of the jar. Based on the state of stomach contents, and the time of Lynne's last meal, the doctors agreed on the time of death. That tight window placed Steven with Lynne when she died. He'd given her a ride on the handlebars of his bicycle, as several witnesses testified. According to Steven, he dropped her off near the highway before turning back toward the base.

Three months after his murder conviction, Steven's appeal was unanimously dismissed by the Ontario courts, but Prime Minister Diefenbaker commuted the teenage boy's death sentence to life imprisonment. In January of 1966, Isabelle LeBourdais, an investigative journalist and author, penned an explosive book that put the Canadian system of jurisprudence on trial. Her reporting suggested Truscott's case had been rushed and sloppy. She raised specific questions about the findings of Dr. Penistan, the pathologist who interpreted stomach contents to extrapolate time of death. The ensuing media frenzy fanned the flames of outrage among a public shaken by the idea that the police and the courts could be fatally flawed.

In April of 1966, based on public pressure, the Government asked the Supreme Court of Canada to review the trial. New experts were recruited to strengthen or refute the testimony of their predecessors. John's mentor, Professor Keith Simpson, was one of those newly drafted experts. His testimony, like Penistan's, proved pivotal in the court's final decision. The other well-known forensic pathologist from the United Kingdom, Dr. Francis Camps, was hired by the defence.

The British doctors travelled to Ontario in the fall of 1966 to testify. They were joined by a raft of experts on either side. Simpson's team boasted veteran doctors from New York City and Ohio, plus the original pathologist, Dr. Penistan. On the defence side, Camps held court with doctors from Baltimore and Toronto. Two continents' worth of experts were facing off in Canada's Supreme Court.

The interpretation of evidence was wildly skewed. Steven's fate bounced back and forth between expert statements. The prosecution, backed by an insistent Dr. Simpson, maintained their stomach contents theory regarding time of death, while the defence and Camps insisted digestion was too varied among individuals and circumstances to indicate anything close to an accurate time of death.

A slender but jowly Simpson began many of his replies with "My lord," and continued to argue in support of Penistan's findings with an affectation of extraneous language.

Camps, a stout and hardy fellow, glared at Simpson from the stand and became ever more aggravated by the prosecution's personal attacks on his character.

After a year of review, the nine-man tribunal of Canada's Supreme Court voted eight-to-one to uphold Truscott's conviction. Simpson had already travelled back to London with his newly polished ego and an immovable wedge stuffed squarely between himself and his colleague Camps.

By the early fall of 1967, around the same time of Truscott's failed attempt to obtain a new trial, young Dr. Butt began his tutelage under Dr. Simpson. John travelled daily on the underground to meet the esteemed doctor wherever the first autopsy of the day was scheduled. At the close of cases from the day's first stop, John, Dr. Simpson, and occasionally Mrs. Simpson, piled into the doctor's car and headed off to the next mystery on the rotation. Mrs. Simpson often brought a thermos of hot tea. The days were usually gruelling, visiting body after body in mortuaries all over the city and countryside. John found the Simpsons terribly kind and generous. Finally, here was a mentor he could admire.

In Simpson's lab at Guy's Hospital, John chatted with another pathology technician.

"How did you end up following Dr. Simpson around the countryside?" the tech asked.

"Well, I'd been attending lectures by Dr. Camps over at the London Hospital and that piqued my interest," John replied. "So I made some enquiries and next thing I know, I'm sitting with Dr. Simpson and he's telling me he's willing to test my aptitude."

The student's eyes grew wide.

Oh jeezus, John thought, *I've stepped in it again*. He had no idea what he might have said wrong.

"If Prof ever hears about you going over to see Camps, you won't be around for long." This professional grudge was John's first glimpse at the ego involved when men of science disagree. He took his new colleague's advice and never mentioned Simpson's nemesis again.

For more than two months, John contentedly shadowed Simpson, one body at a time, until November 5th, when the Sunday evening commuter train from Hastings to Charing Cross went off the rails near the Hither Green maintenance depot in the eastern fringes of London.

There were twelve passenger cars filled to standing room only with young people heading back to the city after a weekend at their family homes on the south coast. Eleven of those cars derailed and crashed into one another with lethal consequences. Surviving passengers reported rocks ricocheting off the sides of the train as it swung into the curved track at 90 miles per hour. The front wheels hit a piece of broken rail as the train rounded the bend. Four cars flipped onto their sides and skidded hundreds of metres before stopping. The first car flipped, rammed by the others behind, and continued on 250 metres further. The broken rail skewered the sideways cars, impaling anything in its path. Crews worked into the night trying to reach survivors. When the recovery effort wrapped up the following day, 49 people were dead and another 78 injured.

In the morning, John met Dr. Simpson at the Borough Mortuary in southeast London. The morgue was a sea of mangled remains. Victims were plentiful and young. For two days he followed Simpson through the systematic analysis of body after body. There were two mysteries to solve here: What do the injuries reveal about the individual's death, and what do the findings show with regard to the accident on a larger scale?

After John's second day among the crushed and pierced bodies, he went back to his tiny apartment and wept openly in front of his wife. But that was the only time. He felt alone. He couldn't talk to Barb about dead bodies. All of his contemporary medical friends were back in Canada. He had to talk himself out of the anguish. Blubbering, as his mother taught him, was for sissies. If he was to pursue a career in forensics, he'd have to stand tall and stiff against the grisly sights and smells. *Be a man*, he lectured himself. By the next morning, he'd successfully stuffed his emotions down and marched back to his post by Prof. Simpson's side.

At the end of the three-month observation period, John found himself once again sitting across from Professor Simpson, discussing the direction of his future.

"Butt, I think you are very observant. I think you have an aptitude for this kind of work."

"You're very kind." Finally, some praise from a successful man of science. John knew he'd found his niche in medicine. Forensic pathology offered a constant supply of mysteries to solve, and he liked to play sleuth with science.

"We could get you into Guy's Hospital if you want to continue with a forensic pathology specialization."

John hadn't expected the offer. He and Barb were planning to tour Europe, and then head back to Canada.

"Without question," John told Simpson. "I want to continue." Britain was the best place to study forensic pathology and John knew for certain it was the right path for him. He knew the decision would put more strain on his already tenuous marriage, and his first child was due to arrive imminently. But he'd finally found his calling, and he needed to chase it down before it got away from him.

The next three years in London were filled with work at Guy's Hospital and pathology studies for John while he continued to perform physicals to earn an income. Barb stopped working after their first child, Jessica, was born in the fall of 1968. Kimberly came only fourteen months later. Barb had her hands full with the kids while John was consumed with his duties. He worked and attended lectures during the week, then abandoned his family and their little flat on the weekends to study in the quiet library at Guy's. In the third year of the forensic program, John was hired as a lecturer in forensic medicine at Charing Cross Hospital, where students from Guy's were given priority for jobs.

John was convinced he could still have a functioning, well-adjusted family. But, as the girls grew, the marriage shrank. Barb had stopped talking to her husband. It seemed to him she'd only speak if he prodded her, answering his questions, but nothing more. It infuriated him. He took off his wedding ring in protest and left it off. Barb didn't say a thing. They continued to wage a silent battle through the summer, until John's father came to visit. Barb was pleasant and loving to Jack, but continued to give John the cold shoulder. It was a huge issue. Isobel and Jack had always been harmonious and happy together. John yearned to show his father the image of a successful family man, but his wife wasn't playing her part.

After his father left, John stood in the small kitchen of their flat. A smoked piece of glass separated him from the living room. Barb stood at the sink and the kids played in the salon on the other side of the glass partition. John was possessed by thoughts of his looming exams, memories of crushing embarrassment in front of his dad, and his apparent impotence to solve the communication issues with his wife. He grabbed a china plate from the counter and smashed it on the floor not far from Barb. The explosion shocked John, as if he didn't know he'd thrown it. He felt as though he was losing control.

In the spring of 1972, when John was preparing to take his forensic pathology exams, the pressure to do well consumed his thoughts. He was almost thirty-eight and had a wife and two children to support. Everything planned for their future hinged on passing the pathology tests and launching his career in earnest. Studying became more difficult. Trouble at home pulled at his thoughts too, making concentration seemingly impossible. He'd ignored his marriage and the family for too long, and he felt his dreams of success slipping through his tightly clenched fists.

John arranged to postpone his exams for a year, then found a marriage counselor through a reference from their family doctor. The consultant psychologist had an expensive practice in Harley Street. John, eager to get things moving and make the most of their limited dollars, took over at the sessions, galloping ahead with his list of woes.

"She won't get out of bed, she's late for everything, she won't talk to me, and—" The anxiety and anger behind his words shook his voice.

"I want you to be quiet and let your wife speak." The counselor tried in vain to make space for Barb. The threesome sat in silence for as many seconds as John was able to hold his tongue. After two sessions with little progress and a lighter wallet, the Butts moved from high-end Harley Street to a family psychiatrist and counseling team at the Maudsley Hospital.

On a Friday night, after a particularly difficult day at work, John decided to walk home and ruminate on his current difficulties. It was a straight route to home, down the old Kent road, three hours on foot. It was cold, and the wet English air wrapped the landscape in fall dampness. He started off from Charing Cross Hospital with his mind fixed on the problems at hand. The monotonous, meditative walk allowed him time to develop a rationale for the domestic dilemma. He wasn't happy, she wasn't happy, and there was no honesty in it. They were spending the time and money to see a counselor and trying to work things out. He had to be utterly honest with her if he expected progress. *I can't keep this up. I have to tell her about the men,* he thought. Integrity was a shield he'd polished for years and he knew the unspoken truth was a tarnishing omission in their marriage.

Once home, John sat Barb down for a talk. Dread mounted his shoulders and smacked his face red. The roar of an ocean plugged his hot ears.

He started plainly. "I had some experiences as a younger man. I had relationships with men. It started with Alex in school when I was a boy, but that felt innocent. And Bill, he seduced me." He didn't tell her everything; she didn't need to know everything.

"When we go back to North America, I'll arrange for us to see Masters and Johnson. He's an OB/GYN, and she's a psychologist. They're highly successful." He thought he'd said enough to get his message across, though Barb gave little response to his admissions. Nothing changed, as far as he could tell.

No matter what he tried, John was unable to reach his wife. She gave him no encouragement, and seemed to be unfazed by his confession. She displayed no desire to see the famous Americans, nor engage in a discussion regarding the issues at hand. They continued in one-sided counseling, getting nowhere.

Fall wore into winter and it became time again to prepare for the Morbid Anatomy and Forensic Pathology exams. The anxiety was at least as bad as before and he hadn't solved a thing since the last testing season. John turned his attention to building images of his future. He needed a job, but not in the UK where competition for key positions was fierce and long. He sent out word of his ensuing credentials to the chosen medical authorities in various locations across North America. Before long, he had an interview in Seattle.

The trip was long and he only stayed for a brief time. The rush of a big American city made his heart race. After seven years in Great Britain, he wasn't used to the hyper pace. Alone in the hotel room with the sound of traffic seeping through the window, sleep wouldn't come. Nothing calmed him and his head buzzed continuously. *What if I fail my exams and I can't take this job? What if I can't get a job?* The interview was a blur. The whole trip was out of focus.

Back at home in the London flat, John sat in his living room exhausted and disoriented. He hadn't heard anything from the Seattle contingent. His anxiety nagged constantly. He stared across the room—white walls, framed posters of famous prints—the room became incongruously large while he and the settee shrank to toy-size in the vastness. As quickly as the illusion came, it vanished. *What is happening to me?* he thought.

Three weeks passed with no relief. The internal buzzing plagued him whenever he didn't get enough rest. He slid out of bed one morning to get ready for work. Something felt wrong. He left Barb asleep in the bed and went to shave. In the bathroom, staring at himself in the mirror, he had a sense of duality. He felt outside of himself, as if he were looking at himself as another, separate person. The buzzing had increased to a roar.

He called the police.

"Something terrible is going to happen in my house. I don't know what it is, but something terrible is going to happen," John told dispatch.

Two police officers arrived at the house minutes later. They took John outside and conducted separate interviews with the married couple.

"We talked to your wife. She told us all of the things you have on the go. You're under a lot of pressure. But you seem fine now."

"I don't feel fine and I don't like this. I want you to take me somewhere."

"Do you want to kill somebody?"

"Of course I don't *want* to kill anybody." John was careful with his words. He felt out of control but detached from the drama. "I don't want to be here. I just don't want to be here."

They loaded John into the back of a police car and drove away. Barb, the flat, and the girls disappeared in the distance.

Chapter Eight

HABEAS CORPUS

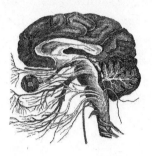

Dire reality dawns early Friday, approximately 36 hours after the plane hit the water. The Medical Examiner has seen everything collected by the people walking the shoreline, the men on the water, and the divers. The remains continue to arrive at a steady pace. Parts, ranging from indiscernible bits to limbs and torsos, fill the bags brought back from the searchers. If there were more intact bodies, they'd have arrived by now. This will take much longer than anticipated.

John can't sleep. It's a dangerous state and he knows it. But this crisis and the work continue, and so does he. Finding help is essential. Qualified medical examiners are few in Canada. Many of the men holding similar positions in other provinces are coroners, and not necessarily forensic pathologists, or even doctors. The pathologists on hand don't have the right experience for the administrative and legal side of the job.

"Get Dr. Young from Ontario," John tells Linda.

John met James Young in 1984 in Scarborough, Ontario, when James was a coroner. By the time Young became the Chief Coroner of Ontario in 1990, John had seen him at several meetings, but hadn't paid much attention to him over the years, except to take note that Young was a general practitioner without any specialization in pathology, and was moving up the ladder nonetheless. Even so, Dr. Butt approves of Dr. Young's work as Ontario's Chief Coroner. James is confident and clearly good at leadership. He is also eloquent, a useful attribute in these tense times. John's only concern is Dr. Young's ambitious ego. According to John, the Coroner seems to think that whatever he is saying should be of great importance to everyone within earshot.

On Friday afternoon, Jeff Katz, the president of Swissair, calls and asks to speak with the Medical Examiner.

"I'd like you to come over to Halifax for a meeting tonight," Katz tells John.

"What's this all about?" John asks. A woman from Swissair had already been in touch with this request and John had turned her down. Now the president is asking.

"We're having an information session for the families, and we'll be meeting at the RCMP headquarters to debrief first. I'd like you to be there."

"Well, I don't think that will work because I'm way over here on the other side of the harbour and I can't spare the time. We're dealing with an unusually complex situation here."

"We'll get a helicopter to bring you over and back." Katz is not going to accept a refusal.

"I suppose so, then. If you think it's necessary for me to be there." *How far can you go in forensic pathology without talking to the family?* John thinks. It's been his philosophy, developed after years of dealing with the grief around death, to put the families of victims first.

Often, there is nothing new to be learned in a death investigation. A heart surgeon can perform the same double bypass hundreds of times with the same enthusiasm because there is a patient's life to save. But what is the impetus for the doctor who performs hundreds of autopsies on victims of cardiac disease? It's always the people who are the most affected by the death who most need the answers. For the grieving, every answer, no matter how simple or medically mundane, is something. An eighteenth century quote from physician and father of modern anatomy Giovanni Morgagni—"This is a place where death delights to help the living"—can be found on the walls of many morgues. Early in his career as a medical examiner, John crafted his personal, more specific, version of the famous adage: *This is the place where our patient is the family.* But he didn't often deliver the findings of autopsies to the loved ones. He had professional medical staff trained specifically to deal with grief and loss. On rare occasions, a family might ask to speak with Dr. Butt. He was willing to see them if he felt they needed to hear something from him to finally accept what the science had offered.

Now, with this demand-request from the airline president, John is expected to confront hundreds of mourners to deliver the worst news, and he has no idea how.

* * *

Over at Bob and Peggy Conrad's, the phone continues to ring with requests for information from news agencies all over the world. Bob can still feel the child's body in his hands and see the mess on the water, but he doesn't want to talk about it. A chasm has opened between the fisherman and his world. He's alone on the other side of a life-altering experience.

A message from Peggy's cousin Raymond in Washington provides the beginnings of a bridge. Monte Wilkins, who died in the plane crash, is the son of Ray's former student, David Wilkins. Ray asks Peggy and Bob to reach out to the Wilkins when they are in Halifax.

Bob puts his hesitations aside and calls the hotel. All of the family members and loved ones, along with those who are there to care for the grieving, are staying at the Lord Nelson Hotel in the heart of Halifax. The Wilkins haven't checked in yet, so Bob leaves a simple message for the family. It feels productive. Somehow, he knows he has a salve to offer, however slight. For the first time since leaving the scene of the crash, since he turned his boat away from the debris field of torn bodies and his grace was supplanted by animal shock, Bob feels grateful to have been there.

* * *

The Lord Nelson Hotel is the point of convergence for the living. Various arms of local and provincial government are busy linking hands, creating a stanchioned path leading the world of mourners to the location of their loss. Nova Scotia Premier Russell MacLellan releases a statement to the press: "This province will open its doors and its arms to those who lost loved ones ..."

MacLellan speaks for the people in the communities touched by the crash when he says it. Nova Scotians are caring people, familiar with lending a hand to those in need, and doing so with the humility that creates ease of acceptance. The Halifax Tourism Department arranges for hundreds of hotel rooms to be vacant and ready.

David and Janet Wilkins deplane with their three remaining children at the Stanfield International Airport, 40 kilometres from Halifax. They board a chartered bus with other families of victims and ride quietly toward downtown, past Dartmouth where Shearwater houses the morgue at Hangar B, over the MacKay Bridge, to the semi-circle driveway and double doors of the Lord Nelson Hotel. The mood on the bus is sombre. Relative silence is punctured by outbreaks of emotion. The ride seems endless to David. He just wants to get his lost son's remains and go home to grieve in private with his family.

By the time the Wilkins arrive, the polished stone and dark wood lobby is already overcrowded with people. Crystal chandeliers and arched windows surround the dishevelled, unwilling travellers. Chairs and benches have no space for more. Two sets of wide marble stairs at either end of the lobby serve as overflow benches, and many people sit on the floor.

The Wilkins find a spot on the carpet while they wait for their room. David and Janet don't want to talk to anyone, though many counselors and spiritual leaders are quietly canvassing the teeming lobby in the event they can offer someone help. Eventually, David is called up for a room assignment and told of an information session for the families that evening at 7 p.m. in the ballroom off the lobby.

Once in their room, David gets the message from Bob Conrad and thinks, *Who on earth is leaving me a message here already?* Despite his desire to keep himself and his immediate family sequestered and safe, he decides to return the call. It strikes him that somebody cared enough to reach out and responding might be a blessing for all involved.

The man on the other end of the phone starts with a straightforward introduction. "You don't know me personally, my name is Bob Conrad. I'm a local fisherman ..." He goes on to explain their connection through Ray, and offers his family's help to the Wilkins in whatever way they might find useful. The two men talk for a few minutes before Bob mentions he'd been on the water looking for survivors. David feels an instant connection. Here is a man who went to the place where Monte was lost, who did what David would have done had he been able. Bob suggests that David and his family come out to the house so they can ask all the questions they want, and Bob will give them any answers he has.

* * *

Linda doesn't envy Dr. Butt's task tonight. She believes that the ME's office is paid to focus on the dead, not mollycoddle all the relatives. Handholding is not in her job description. It's bad enough that she has to walk through an alley of plywood autopsy suites to take a bathroom break. The smell gets worse every day. This job is getting crazy.

The calls to Hangar B from families, and anyone other than officials with the internal phone list, come first to a phone bank staffed by the RCMP. When a grief-stricken man calls from Italy, he gets patched through to Linda by accident. She can make out some of what he's saying, but he won't stop crying, and that's making it harder. She tells him there are no answers yet, but he keeps going and going.

"Listen," Linda says, "we're here working, doing everything we can to identify everybody. We're treating everybody with respect, and we really feel for the families. But we have to get on with it."

After the ambush questioning, Linda calls everyone around Hangar B. "Don't ever put calls from the family through to me again. That's not my job. If I have to start dealing with the families, I cannot do this job."

* * *

At RCMP headquarters, John sits in a room full of powerful men, all leaders in their various organizations: admirals, superintendents, directors, a president, and a chief officer. The cadre discusses what information it has to share with the families. John hardly hears any of it. The adrenaline-induced buzzing in his head blurs their talking points, and he hardly remembers a blind bit of it by the time they are en route to the hotel. *What am I going to say to these people?* The question takes up all of the John's thinking capacity.

The group of disaster officials arrives at the Lord Nelson shortly before 7 p.m. People swarm on the sidewalk around the hotel, funneling toward the glass-paned doors at the top of the round driveway. Well-marked security guards shoo reporters away from the scene. The group of official men is shuttled through the crowd without incident.

The lobby is packed cheek by jowl. At a bank of cubicles tucked along the side of the room, family members are gently asked to share information to help identify their loved ones. Soft-spoken professionals and volunteers ask about broken bones, x-rays, dental records, and doctors' names. They ask about hairbrushes, and toothbrushes, and anything that might contain DNA. They ask for blood samples from those related to the victims. The scene is a world away from the workings of the morgue. John never thought, as he was elbow-deep in his work, that he'd be facing hundreds of family members less than forty-eight hours post-disaster. Walking through the melee of grieving loved ones, he wonders what solace he can possibly offer. The makeshift morgue at Shearwater houses more horror than he has seen in his many years working with death. How will he address the families without divulging too many of the dreaded details?

Swissair President Jeff Katz leads the group to the ballroom entrance on the far side of the lobby at the top of the low stairs. Without much conversation, they mount a platform at the front of the room and arrange themselves on chairs in a semicircle while the reluctant audience settles in for the debriefing. This sea of people resembles the scene of the crash. Signs of devastation float on the surface and hint at the greater wreckage beneath. Hundreds of people fill the large space, with the families and their caregivers making up the entire crowd. No reporters linger on the edges of the room, no bright lights or cameras point at the officials on stage, no recorders catch sound bites for the never-ending cycle of news. This session is for the loved ones only.

Jeff Katz starts the debriefing. He gives general information about the flight, such as its planned trajectory, point of departure, and time of final communication. He also pledges ongoing support to the grief-stricken while they endure this tragedy.

The Navy Admiral talks about the aborted rescue mission that turned into a recovery operation when no survivors were found. The various authoritative men on the platform speak to the contribution of vessels, helicopters, planes, trucks, and manpower. RCMP Command skirts around the distribution of any hard data, commensurate with their constant and necessary suspicion this crash may be the result of a crime. Each man on stage gives a report about his area of expertise. They talk of the investigation into a cause, of the systems in place to recover and record, of doing everything that can be done to answer the questions at hand.

John is the last to speak. He wasn't able to take in much of what the others have said. He's overwhelmed. Tender shoots of empathy have grown in his stomach, winding out in all direction like an invasive vine, choking out any sense of calm or control.

"I deeply regret what I have to tell you today...." He starts slowly, offering condolences, brushing against the catastrophe he has come to address.

John feels the other men on stage tense at his earnestness. He knows what is expected of him in his position as a man of science and a master of death, but he can't do it. He won't be hard against anguish this time.

Tears threaten. He feels the lump forming in his throat. In this moment, the Medical Examiner can be nothing but nakedly honest, his previously impervious protective shell on the floor at his feet. All of the bullshit with bureaucracy, with ego and jurisdiction, with scientific interpretation, with what the neighbours think, and who knows, and whom he loves—it all falls away while he stands at the podium and gazes over the physical manifestation of agony. This decision to be frank and honest is also a decision to let go and weep while several of his peers, all of whom spoke with calm detachment, watch him lose control.

He continues. "I'm so very sorry to have to tell you that none of you will ever see your loved ones again."

The magnitude of this confession is transformative. The audience comes alive with distress. Some people faint, others wail. The stage cadre appears confused, or at least surprised.

John takes his seat.

Mr. Katz opens the floor for questions. Most are directed at the Medical Examiner. Here, as last, is the man who may have seen their lost loves, may have touched them, may even have them somewhere in a cold place, waiting to be brought home. They press Dr. Butt for specific answers.

"Where is my mother father brother sister child?"

"Where are the bodies?"

"Where? Where? WHERE?"

John tries to find a way, amidst the outcries, to gently indicate the state of affairs. "The force of the crash was such that its impact with the water, uhhh, that the plane did not remain intact. We are still in the early stages of identification because of the nature of this terrible accident. It will take months to positively identify everyone who was on the flight."

The audience continues to hold its collective breath, waiting for something definitive, staring intently at the man on stage.

"There will be little opportunity for visual identification," John says. The people refuse to accept his subtle answers, but he desperately wants to spare them the grisly details.

He tries another approach. "We have seen only one intact body."

There is a moment of stunned silence. Then the one body becomes the focus. The audience demands to know who it is.

"In the interest of identification, I can tell you it is the body of a Black woman." John hopes this meeting can, at least, provide him with one positive ID before the night is over.

* * *

In the audience, David and Janet Wilkins sit with their adult children. They feel the tension in the room with so much anguish in one place. David knows his son is dead and the people around him are suffering something similar, though they are from many backgrounds with different beliefs. Everyone is here, like him, to collect the lost and lay them to rest in peace.

The Wilkins are moved by Dr. Butt's gentle voice and quiet patience. They hear compassion in the Medical Examiner's voice, which they hadn't noticed when the other men spoke. It isn't what David expects from a hard-nosed pathologist. This man on stage is grieving with them. It feels like he is holding the whole room in his hands. David can see that Dr. Butt is struggling through tears, and it's horribly soothing.

The ME's stark words quiet the crowd. Calmness, like oil on tumultuous waters, restores the earlier stillness while the news sinks slowly to the bottoms of their hearts—no intact bodies, save one. Mr. Katz finishes the formal meeting with an announcement that each of the men on stage will stay after to answer any private questions. A long, disorganized queue forms around John. David Wilkins works his way over to the messy line and waits for a turn. There is another blessing to share here.

The crowd around John grows. Many of the mourners are reaching out, touching the ME's shoulder, running a hand down the sleeve of his suit coat and squeezing his arm, or patting him gently on the back. They seem to need physical contact with the man who will care for their lost loved ones, as if forming a final physical connection to the dead. They also seem to be consoling him.

* * *

"I'm Dr. David Wilkins from Loma Linda, California," the man says, shaking John's hand. "I lost my youngest child, my son Monte, in this tragedy."

"I'm so sorry to hear that," John replies, while shaking the man's hand.

Dr. Wilkins puts his arm around John's shoulder. "I'm concerned about how you are holding up. I can see that you're speaking to us from your heart. This is all putting quite a strain on you."

John feels the heat move up his face again, and the tears return. This perfect stranger who lost his son is offering counsel to the man who delivered the worst news moments ago. David's generosity and compassion in this moment of distress are like nothing John has experienced before, and he is broken open again by the exchange. The entire evening has seen his years of carefully constructed reserve crumble to dust and wash away.

CHAPTER NINE

HOMECOMING

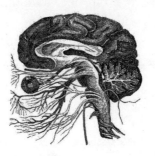

GUY'S HOSPITAL SITS near the south end of London Bridge, across the River Thames from John's flat by Regent's Park. Many important men have walked the corridors of Guy's since the hospital was founded in 1721. Thomas Addison discovered the adrenal gland disease that bears his name. John Braxton Hicks, Thomas Hodgkin, and even the romantic poet John Keats, all spent time at Guy's Hospital.

John hadn't been back since he left two years before to take a post at Charing Cross Hospital completing autopsy upon autopsy, working under yet another unlikeable man. It had been the final stage of his training. Looking across Guy's antiquated courtyard, approaching the stone arches and pillars of the façade in the back of a police car, John felt fear. One of his colleagues might see him. Arriving at this familiar place with a police escort was disconcerting, but once admitted to the psych ward, he felt relief, despite the bars on the windows and the shame of a possible encounter.

After an assessment, where he spoke at length about his wife, his exams, and his curious perceptions of watching himself from the outside, the psychiatrist prescribed haloperidol, a hefty antipsychotic, and chloral hydrate for sleep. John refused the haloperidol. He didn't want to be under the influence of mind-altering medications with his exams only days away. He was writing those exams, come hell or high water. The sleeping pills, however, provided a welcome relief. Finally, he slept soundly through the night. But no diagnosis was forthcoming.

Down the hall, there was a young ghost of a girl suffering from anorexia. She hardly came out of her room. John approached her quietly and connected with her easily. The pair spent hours in quiet conversation. The doctors expressed surprise. She hadn't spoken in weeks. No one had been able to gain her confidence. Her acceptance of his kindness was a soothing balm for John's jangled nerves. His sensitivity could help people. There were two sides to this emotional coin.

After a brief battle with the psychiatrist, John had his medical books brought to the ward and went back to studying with few interruptions. Barb wasn't able to visit with two little children in tow, and John didn't tell anyone what was happening, other than his prick of a boss, out of necessity. He didn't know when he'd return to work. But, shortly after his intake, John got a day pass from the psych ward and left the hospital in the morning to write his pathology exams, returning in the evening before the sun went down. After two years of constant anxiety about the tests, he passed.

The psychiatrists assured John's boss at Charing Cross that this episode was the result of exhaustion and stress. After his discharge, John went right back to performing autopsies and searching for new job opportunities. He wanted to go home, back to the new world of possibilities. The UK was well stocked with forensic pathologists. North America was not.

John asked a friend to connect him with Professor Lannigan, the head of pathology at the new University of Calgary Medical School at Foothills Hospital. Lannigan had moved from the UK to Calgary in 1969 to head up the department at the new med school. John wouldn't have to explain the benefits of a properly trained forensic pathologist to a Scotsman. All UK doctors were well versed on the subject. After a brief trip to Calgary and a successful interview, an invigorated Dr. Butt planned to finally move his family home.

Only weeks later, when John had returned to London from his

interview, he received a letter from the Alberta Medical Association. They wanted his ideas on building a medical examiner system in the province, and he happily provided them with all of his thoughts in a return correspondence. *Well, that's encouraging!* he thought.

By January of 1974, less than one year after John's hospitalization, he'd moved Barb and the girls across the ocean and back to his hometown to start a new job as Associate Professor of Pathology for the University of Calgary. Fourteen years after graduating from medical school, he'd found his place in the system and was ready and determined to do great things. At the time, he was the only qualified forensic pathologist in Western Canada. Three hours drive north of his new post, at the University Hospital of Alberta in Edmonton where John went to med school, and where the province's Chief Coroner had his office, some of the doctors and administrators were feeling rankled by the new upstart and his highbrow training. The government, however, had high hopes for young Dr. Butt, and they reached out to him a few months after his return from the UK.

In Canada, each province or territory is responsible for its own death-scene investigations. Most Canadian provinces, and all of the territories, use a coroner system. When John arrived in Calgary, the Chief Coroner, Dr. Max Cantor, an MD working out of the University Hospital in Edmonton, ran the Coroner's Office for the Government of Alberta. A fundamental difference between a coroner system and a medical examiner system lies with the credentials of the leader. Medical examiners must be doctors, preferably forensic pathologists, while coroners can come up through the ranks of the police force, through the justice system, from the political realm, or via several other professional trajectories. No specific medical credentials are required for the post of coroner. The two types of offices are also governed by different legal acts, though both offices have the same over-arching mandate: death investigation for the people. In the early seventies, Alberta's economy was gushing and the government took pride in investing in its systems and structure. They wanted to be the best at everything. At the time, only Manitoba, Nova Scotia, and Newfoundland and Labrador used the medical examiner system. Alberta's judiciary review panel, known as the Kirby Board of Review, issued a report in 1973 recommending the province switch systems.

Dr. Maxwell Mordecai Cantor, a thin man with a prominent chin and little hair, hailed from Winnipeg, Manitoba, where he'd been born in 1903 and completed his education as a doctor in 1929. Cantor had garnered considerable attention for his successful role as Chief Coroner in Alberta, a position he'd held for nearly 30 years before young Dr. Butt arrived on the medical-legal scene. In 1972, Cantor had been awarded the Government of Alberta Achievement Award for his work in forensic medicine. He'd received a Canadian Centennial Medal in 1967, and Red Cross Gold Medal in 1941, and he was the absolute death authority in the province of Alberta, until John arrived.

In June of 1974, five months after his start at the Foothills Hospital, John received a phone call from the Deputy Minister of Community Health, Bill Cochrane, the former dean at the University of Calgary Medical School. Cochrane had interviewed John the previous year. "The Public Commissioner is interested in talking with you. He wants to talk about the future of forensic pathology in the province."

Holy Crap! John thought. He knew what was coming.

Within the week, the Alberta government brought the young forensic pathologist up to Edmonton to meet with Attorney General Merv Leitch. Mr. Leitch was also a native Calgarian, and had been a lawyer in the city for years before moving to politics, and the province's capitol, in 1971. Although they didn't know one another, he and John were contemporaries.

"I assume you know about the Kirby Report?" Leitch asked John.

"I received a letter about it from the Alberta Medical Association when I was in Great Britain."

"I wonder if you would consider looking at it?"

John suspected this question might be posed to him. He also knew the AG's subtle question was a thinly veiled job offer. On one hand, John had made a commitment to the administration at Foothills

Hospital, the University of Calgary, and the doctors who had hired him. On the other hand, if he didn't do it, somebody else would. Why pass up the opportunity to design an entire system from the ground up? This was his chance to really do something important, to make his mark.

"I'll do it," he told Leitch. "Without question. I'll do it."

Life was falling into place. Even his marriage seemed a little better. There had been so many arrangements to make preparing for the move back to Canada, Barb was forced to communicate with him. Dealing with logistics created common concerns and problems they were able to solve as a team. After they packed up their home, the family took a vacation in Bermuda, then flew to Toronto. Barb went on to Calgary to get their new home together while John did a quick tour of medical examiner facilities in the US. He didn't know at the time how useful that fact-finding mission would be.

John threw himself into work, continuing his job at the Foothills Hospital while building a medical examiner system from scratch. His new position as future Chief ME threw the other, established doctors into a tizzy. John was in hot water with both the University Hospital in Edmonton, where Dr. Cantor was stationed, and at the Medical School in Calgary.

Months passed while John worked with lawyers to draft provincial legislation. His stress level inched up as the sleepless nights passed. Barb wasn't interested in his evening rants, either. She didn't seem to want to hear about his fights with the hospitals and the other doctors. She was building a new life of her own, back at school completing a degree in nursing. They didn't have much time to socialize, but the couple managed to attend the occasional dinner party. It seemed to John that Barb was often tremendously late, to the point where they started taking separate cars. He'd go on first and make excuses for Barb's absence. Her disregard for time embarrassed and infuriated him. After the cross-Atlantic move brought a brief respite from the silence, the couple reverted back to limited communication and growing tension in day-to-day cohabitation. John had to stay focused on his career. Once the ME system was in place, he'd devote more time to solving his troubles on the home front. For now, the problems at work took precedence.

The Chief Coroner in Edmonton, Dr. Cantor, had placed himself squarely against the new medical examiner system. Once John became the province's Chief ME, Cantor's role as the premiere death investigator for Alberta would disappear. John wasn't doing anything to facilitate a relationship with Dr. Cantor, and he wasn't about to tolerate what he considered this Chief Coroner's outdated and inappropriate procedures.

In November of 1975, Edmonton's former mayor, William Hawrelak, passed away peacefully in bed during the night. The mayor's cause of death, cardiac disease, was announced on the radio the next morning. John was incensed. *Did the family even know? Were they hearing it on the radio for the first time, too? Who the hell is giving out information to the media?* He called the Edmonton University Hospital public affairs office.

"This is a Coroner's case," John ranted to a PR liaison. "It's totally inappropriate for information to be released by the University Hospital!" He realized that Dr. Cantor was sharing private coroner investigation information with the hospital, and John wasn't going to stand for it.

Within an hour, Dr. Bernard Snell, another Scotsman and the President of the Edmonton University Hospital, called back to put the younger doctor in his place. "I don't want you ringing here and talking to my staff. I don't want you directing any people here about what they are going to do or not do."

John had been a student of Dr. Snell in his early medical school years, and he remembered the man's disposition. He thought, *Let it go, just let it go.* He didn't argue. But he didn't forget either.

After a bit more digging, John discovered the University Hospital doctors were asking families to consent to autopsies on their loved ones. If they didn't agree, the University doctors might tell the family that the Coroner's Office would probably order an autopsy anyway. What the families likely didn't know was how the information might be handled if the autopsy results were the property of the hospital, and not the coroner. Hospitals used the information as they saw fit—for studies, to generate data, even to promote their authority by announcing the cause of a local politician's death. Coroners and MEs operate under different rules of conduct, and the information they gather is kept private unless it's needed in a legal matter.

They'd gone too far. Men of medicine and justice cannot and must not manipulate the vulnerable they are meant to protect. John insisted the practice of bullying families for information had to stop. He drew his battle lines. "When the new law is enacted, these autopsy reports must be sanctioned by the Office of the Chief Medical Examiner. If you want a copy of it for someone who has died on your premises, or in your emergency room, you'll have to request it. The hospital has no right to the thing." The fight was on.

Dr. Cantor and the old guard mounted a campaign to crush the new kid. It was easy to get the older doctors on board. They didn't like the idea of any medical or academic authority in the province moving south to Calgary where John intended to house the Office of the Chief ME. They also didn't like John. But when Cantor tried to rally the police in Calgary against the soon-to-be Medical Examiner, he didn't get any traction.

The Chief of Police went straight to the incumbent's successor, "Doc, the Chief Coroner up in Edmonton is saying you're not in charge. He says we shouldn't be cooperating with you."

Officially, there was no law backing John's authority. The Chief Coroner was, legally, still in charge. But the new system, one that made Cantor obsolete, was inevitable, regardless how much the old doctor writhed against it.

Dr. Butt took Cantor's correspondence up the chain of command to the Deputy Minister. The anticipated result meant more work for John. The Minister relieved Dr. Cantor as Chief Coroner, and bestowed the title on John. Cantor was offered a consulting position within the department, though the intended olive branch did little to appease the deposed leader. Cantor wasn't ready to give up.

Months prior to Cantor's dismissal, in the spring of 1975, the North Saskatchewan River ice broke with the thaw and a body washed up at Elk Point, east of Edmonton. The RCMP were called to the scene and the remains sent to a hospital in Edmonton for examination. Though the body was badly decomposed, the RCMP were able to obtain fingerprint evidence. At the time, all analyses of fingerprints utilized a hand-held magnifying glass and a sharp eye. The individual making the comparison of loops and whorls had to be decisive.

The RCMP identification team concluded the man was a former civic politician from Edmonton who had been missing for several months. The Mounties drove to the missing man's home and told his wife that her husband had turned up dead. A funeral service transpired, where his many friends and family shed tears and moved from their grief of the unknown to certain sadness.

Spring turned to summer, and John had taken over as the Chief Coroner just before an Edmonton City Police Officer decided he had to speak out. He didn't agree with the RCMP investigator's assessment of identity. To him, there weren't enough similarities in the fingerprint from the cadaver and the one the city police had on file for the missing politician. The disgruntled Edmonton City Police Officer went to the press and a story was printed about the possible misidentification, which was how John found out about the whole kerfuffle. He wasn't having any sloppy work during his watch.

After the body was exhumed, John received the unfortunate news—the RCMP got it wrong. As the Chief Coroner, it was his job to deal with the mess of a misidentification. The remains belonged to a drifter, not the missing politician.

This was John's first experience dealing face to face with the bereaved to deliver difficult news. It didn't occur to him to try and cover anything up. *Well, there's only one way to handle this. I've got to go and talk to his wife*, John thought.

First, he called the RCMP Chief Superintendent. "I'm going to visit this woman in her home and I'd like to think that I have some sort of apology to give to her from the RCMP."

"The way I see it, Dr. Butt, your people signed a death certificate with the wrong identification on it. We didn't do that, your office did."

"Well, yes, and I'm headed out there to offer an apology, and I think the RCMP owes an apology as well. Your people were the ones who misinterpreted the fingerprints and told the poor woman her husband was dead."

"The RCMP never apologize, Doctor."

John felt indignant, and flummoxed. So far, he'd had great relationships with police officers. Shortly after he was asked to create the medical examiner system, the Calgary Police Department asked him to teach classes on forensic investigation tactics. He thought the officers were willing and eager to learn. This guy was a whole different story. John immediately stiffened. He had no cards to play here, but he'd expected decency, at least. The rebuff was filed under "RCMP" in his mind and he adjusted his thinking accordingly.

The stacks of slights were piling up around John while he fought to hold onto everything. Dr. Snell and Dr. Cantor were still working hard to discredit his authority. After he became the Chief Coroner, he was invited to attend grand rounds at the university hospital. *Perhaps they're getting used to me*, he thought. Any department can put on a case in the large amphitheatre. Using "grand" to define the presentation indicates that all of the other departments are invited to attend. At the crucial moment, where the doctors were about to disclose the key piece of information in the case, the cause of death, they stopped and stared at Dr. Butt.

"Unfortunately, we can't give you any official results on this case, because Dr. Butt won't allow us to have a copy of the autopsy report," the lead presenter announced to theatre full of John's peers.

John turned red. Here he was standing among many men who had been his professors in medical school. They were older, established, and in cahoots. This game of calling him out for protecting the privacy of the dead continued at other hospitals where he was invited for lectures. John put his head down and persevered. The law that he helped create would soon come to fruition and then they'd all have to shut the hell up.

Monday to Wednesday, Dr. Butt worked on building the medical examiner system in Calgary, then flew to Edmonton to keep the

Coroner's Office running. He slept less and less while traversing the centerline of Alberta, up and down, over and over. He flew between the two urban centers: Edmonton, where the artists and working men with dirty hands lived; and Calgary, where the dining was fine and the money flowed like oil from the pump jack.

By the summer of 1976, the new *Fatality Enquiries Act of Alberta*, written to govern the new Office of the Chief Medical Examiner, had passed first and second readings in the legislature. The Attorney General decided to let the law lie fallow for a year and allow the community to comment. In the meantime, John had a solid blueprint to start building the physical components of his system. The Deputy Minister decided it was time to hire an Assistant Chief Medical Examiner to lead the Edmonton Office. Dr. Peter Markesteyn, an anatomical pathologist from Rotterdam, was working in Newfoundland while trying to get a position anywhere to the west. John had heard his name before, and agreed to hire Markesteyn as his Deputy, despite what John thought of his questionable credentials. In John's opinion, only an experienced forensic pathologist was good enough, but he was too busy to fuss about it now.

The time had come to start on the design of the actual buildings. John was meticulous in his planning and he intended to have the best state-of-the-art facilities possible. Shortly after Dr. Markesteyn was installed in Edmonton, John planned a whirlwind, four-day trip across the USA to consult with other Medical Examiners and look at their facilities. He took three architects with him, each specializing in different areas of design, and left Peter behind to keep things running smoothly.

John also instituted a review panel to prepare for the changeover of the inquest system. Under the coroner system, the Chief not only investigated the death, but also presided over the public inquest into the circumstances of the death; similar to the way the police and RCMP investigate themselves. The medical examiner system separated the two tasks with a Fatality Review Board choosing which cases required a hearing in front of a provincial court judge. Peter was not invited to sit on the board. John thought that was his job, as the Chief. He was the head administrator, not Markesteyn.

Not even a year had passed before Peter was in front of the Deputy Minister complaining about his controlling boss. Markesteyn felt he should be in charge of the northern office and be included in all important aspects of the medical examiner system.

John was called in for a meeting with the Minister. "Why didn't you have Peter on that trip to the United States?"

"There was nothing for him to do. I was there with three architects to facilitate their visit. We didn't need him with me, we need him here while I was absent."

"He feels he isn't being recognized, that the job was misrepresented to him, and he wants to become the Chief Medical Examiner for Northern Alberta."

"What will you tell him?"

"Never going to happen," the Deputy Minister told John. "But we need to deal with him."

As John was pondering the issue of his discontented number two, and how to appease him, the problem solved itself. When the Deputy told Dr. Markesteyn there was no chance of a Chief ME position for him, that he would always need to report to Dr. Butt, he quit. But Dr. Markesteyn was a harbinger of things to come.

Finally, in July of 1977, the new legislation empowering the Office of the Chief Medical Examiner in Alberta officially became law. John sat on his medical-legal throne at the top of the death investigation pyramid in Alberta. He was finally in control.

CHAPTER TEN

IDENTITY

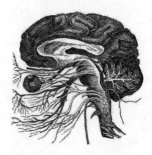

MATTER IS MORPHED by its environment, but never lost. When air and spark cause wood to burn, energy is released as hot gas. But the wood is irrevocably changed. It becomes smoke and ash. Weight and velocity meet a watery wall of stillness and the identities of 229 people crash into one another, breaking apart and coming together, losing themselves in an explosion with the sea. Bringing them back to whole is as impossible as turning ash and smoke into wood.

The people recovering human remains struggle with procedural questions they may never have expected. How small of a piece is too small? Where do they stop? What is enough? At Shearwater, John grapples with these questions as well. The Medical Examiner's job here, according to the government and the budget, is to identify everyone on the plane. But the families want more, and John, at the moment, is the inadvertent arbiter of those expectations.

On Saturday at the morgue, three days after the crash, two blasts of a hand-pumped foghorn announce an all-hands morning quarters at 8:30 a.m. The past two days at Shearwater opened with a meeting of leaders from each area—RCMP, DNA, X-ray, dental, photography, transportation and safety, and so on—for a quick debrief of the past 24 hours. But today John wants to rally all of the troops.

As they muster, a Canadian Air Force psychologist approaches John with a request. "I'm wondering if you would say something about the availability of critical-incident stress management?"

A portable housing unit next to the hangar serves as a lounge and rest area for the staff. Psychologists, counselors, and spiritual leaders have set up there, ready to give support to these people living in a nightmare.

"Certainly. No question. I can address that," John replies. He intends to give a supportive talk, and the psychologist's request dovetails nicely with his plan.

Once the legion has gathered, John begins. "I met with the families last night, and, let me tell you, they are in the grips of despair. Intensely sad. They want their loved ones returned. You can all see by this point that their wish cannot be fulfilled."

The crowd falls silent with the introduction of this unexpected topic. John pauses to collect himself and continues.

"You are the only people who will see and handle these remains. So I want you all to remember that you are representatives of these families. This job we're doing is very important, and you need to know that your role here matters a great deal." He wants the weight of his words to rally them with purpose.

Talking about feelings wasn't in John's initial definition of his work. During the disasters he's worked in the past, John insisted to himself that counseling was for the weak. Regular people needed comfort. Professionals doing their jobs were meant to be immune. Over the years, he's learned to accept help. He recognizes the buzzing in his head as a precursor to a much louder roar, and the downward spiral that ensues. Acknowledging the difficulties, providing support, and encouraging conversations about feelings are all key in keeping the morgue running efficiently, without producing even more casualties.

Walking the morgue floor after the meeting, the Medical Examiner chats with a Catholic chaplain who ministers to the Halifax police. John effuses praise for his team and all of the willing volunteers.

"Well, you know why the atmosphere here is so good, Doctor? It's the souls. There are so many here, holding you up while you put them to rest."

John isn't a fan of philosophizing on spirituality, but his lifetime of tangential connection to the practices surrounding death has taught him to be tolerant and listen. He might learn something.

* * *

Linda's worried. Dr. Butt doesn't have a peer. He's alone up there on top of his hill. Maybe he's out of control, too. What's he doing with the families getting all teary-eyed? That's not his job. Besides, there's too much work to do. People think he's the last connection to their dearly departed, but he's not even doing autopsies!

Yesterday, when she called Dr. Young in Ontario, she was relieved to hear him say yes, and offer to bring his team. Even better, he'll be arriving any minute, and it can't be too soon. Another family call, this time from a grieving mother, was misdirected to Linda's desk. This kind of thing has to stop. She can't let this place get bogged down in drama. Somebody has to reel it in.

Dr. Young is the Chief Coroner of Ontario. The problem is, this Ontario guy isn't a forensic pathologist, so her boss doesn't see Young as an exact equal. According to Linda, Dr. Butt thinks he's better than nearly everyone. Forensic pathologists are not a collaborative group. Their reputations depend on being right, but scientific evidence can invite more than one interpretation. It's like a riddle with many answers, but only one truth. Linda hopes Dr. Butt will put his ego aside and let Dr. Young help with the decision-making.

* * *

Confirmation of victim identities brings a new and difficult need to interact with the families. Dr. Butt, with his fresh connection to the grief stricken, takes on the task of delivering the news, one difficult phone call at a time. He can still see the room of contorted faces from last night. Their questions echo in his ears.

After a day at Shearwater, Butt and his new aide-de-camp, James Young, climb into a car and head across the water to Halifax. John sits on the platform at the front of the ballroom in the Lord Nelson Hotel for a second night. The crowd feels different. Grief is still throbbing, loud and distorted, drowning out most other intentions. But there is a new tension. Yesterday, many were confused, shocked, disoriented. Tonight, they seem angry. They accuse the men on stage of lies by omission. Why does the media seem to know more than them? On Saturday morning, the press reported that a certain number of victims had been identified. John has no idea how the media found an inside source, and he's awfully annoyed about it.

* * *

On Sunday morning, Deputy Minister Gordon Gillis arrives at Shearwater. Linda gives him a hug, as do several others. Some people cry when they see him. He's in a position to fix things, and he's come to do just that. Everything is urgent.

They're desperate for more plywood but the Home Depot is closed on Sunday. "Take the RCMP, have them log everything you remove. Break in." Authorized.

Communication is a major issue. They need cell phones, plenty and fast. But the phone company is structured for long contracts and refuses to supply phones for a short but indefinite period. Gordon calls the head guy and says, "Look, I can't tell you how wonderful everyone has been in this province. We've come together. Michelin donated 10,000 dollars. Everybody's outpouring of generosity has been terrific."

"Thank you," the phone guy replies, not perceiving the set-up.

"Except for yours," Gordon drops the hammer he has poised neatly above the man's neck. "Someday, we'll do an ad, and we'll list them all, and say 'except for Maritime Tel & Tel.'" He waits a beat to see how far he needs to go.

Silence.

Gord continues. "Your people say we can't get these phones be-cause you won't let us have them on immediate need. You want us to go through a form-filling process? We need them NOW. We need them yesterday. And we don't know for how long. We'll pay, I don't care if it's $700 or $7000. We need those phones!"

The threat hangs between them like the red mark at the center of a tug-of-war rope. But Gordon knows he's the winner. He knew it before he made the call.

"Consider it done," the phone guy says.

* * *

The threshold for identification in forensics can be microscopic, but a broken heart needs more evidence to accept the truth of death, and will refuse what it can refute. In the case of a crash as severe as this, DNA evidence recovered from the site is used to prove identity, and therefore, death. It follows that a body, in this situation, cannot necessarily be produced and is not required to issue a death certificate. But those who have lost whole people are hard pressed to believe a few cells can represent an entire individual.

In the Jewish Orthodox tradition, the absence of a body after death creates issues, specifically for wives. Proof of death requires a vital part of the whole, like a heart or a brain. Limbs won't do, pieces of flesh and bone won't do, so a microscopic bit of biological matter used for DNA identification certainly will not do. Women can only be released from marriage with the approval of their husbands, or in the event of death. The penalty for infidelity is extreme. A suppos-edly dead husband's reappearance ruins the life of his wife if she has remarried. According to her religion's laws, a cheating woman must be abandoned by both husbands, and left with a life of shame. No one wants that, so the community strives to find solutions.

Edward Gluck is a Jewish Orthodox Rabbi with a long beard and classic black hat. The Gluck family settled in the Bronx after leaving Germany in the late 1930s when Edward was two years old.

His accent is a mix of Yiddish singsong and punchy consonants from the Boroughs. Rabbi Gluck made it his life's work to create space for the Orthodox Jewish Community. He was instrumental in the incorporation of a Hasidic village in New York, and he fought with fervour to maintain traditional customs. Now, Rabbi Gluck seems determined to take on the role of shepherding the Jewish victims of Swissair 111 back to some kind of wholeness.

On September 2, 1998, the same day that Flight 111 crashed into the sea, the pilots of Air Canada, the nation's largest carrier, went on strike. The walkout created a problem for Swissair and the victims' families. Fortunately, the pilots agree to make concessions, and a shuttle is arranged between New York and Halifax to fly family members and others involved from the States to Canada. Rabbi Gluck and his associate, Rabbi Krupka, are on the Sunday flight.

At Shearwater, John is breathing a little easier with Dr. Young around. The Coroner is proving valuable—intelligent and good at giving instructions. It's September sixth, John's 64th birthday, and he's feeling a bit lonesome for friends. He wants some attention, or celebration, but it's not possible in the midst of this mess. Linda appears at the door of his boardroom office and pulls him back from his reverie.

"The Air Canada Station Manager in Halifax is on the phone for you. Do you have a minute to talk to him?" she asks.

"About what?"

"I'll put him through. You'll want to talk to him."

John might develop a cauliflower ear with all of this time on the phone. The handset feels like a permanent growth on the side of his head.

"We've had a call from the Captain of the aircraft that's flying in, and we think you ought to know about it. Your name is really being bounced around in the cabin of the aircraft."

"Uh, I see." John has no idea what this is about.

The Air Canada manager continues with his story. "The cabin staff picked up on it and told the Captain. I just want you to be prepared, because there's a rabbi on the plane who is really giving your name a bad time."

John thinks, *Well, so what else is new?* "I'm not surprised. But thank you for your call. We'll deal with it when he arrives."

It's bad enough he has to spend his birthday at the Lord Nelson Hotel, the epicenter of sadness, now he has a mad rabbi to deal with, too. Young suggests the two of them go for a late dinner after the meeting, and blow off some steam over a drink or two to celebrate. It lifts John's spirits. Then he gets called to the rest lounge. The Canadian Air Force psychologist arranged it yesterday, after the morning meeting. It's a birthday surprise. Someone has a camera. John sits on a couch beaming at the lens, rosy-cheeked and grinning widely. He's wearing classic blue-green scrubs and runners, with his facemask pulled down, resting on his chin like a paper beard. His smile implies an impish innocence, despite his mature age. In his hand, there's a paper plate with a slice of birthday cake.

Later, in the lobby of the Lord Nelson, John spots a thin, young rabbi standing by one of the ornate wooden columns. He wants to get this confrontation over with, so he strides up to the man in the black hat.

"Are you Rabbi Gluck?"

"No, I'm Rabbi Moshe Krupka."

"I'm Dr. Butt."

"Pleased to meet you. I came with Rabbi Gluck. We're hoping to speak with you. Can we have a meeting?"

"Sure, but let us get over this meeting with the families first."

"We'd like to meet immediately when it's over."

"Fine, there is no problem with that." He walks away with a bad feeling. *This is going to be prickly.*

John sits on stage for a third, and final, night. The other officials have softened. They deliver more details using less officious language, but John is the crowd favourite. He speaks last and is asked the most questions. The demanding tone from the audience has dissipated. John is not an official on the other side of a line. Through empathy and tenderness, through his words and actions, he's become a friend to the grieving crowd.

After the official talk, a long line forms in front of John as he descends from the stage. The questions are easier to answer now as expectations have changed. But there is one obviously agitated man in the line. Another rabbi, an older, stern-faced man in the iconic hat sticking his head out, goose-necking to make eye contact. John apologizes to the next person in line. "I think I better go and talk to this gentleman. I think I better do that right away."

In a few paces, he stands next to Gluck, ready to deal with the autopsy issue head on. He's not angry, but anxious. Before he can start, the rabbi jumps in.

"Dr. Butt, I wish to apologize to you."

Perhaps the rabbi's experience in the crowd that night, listening to the Medical Examiner talk with compassion, and patiently answer the families' questions, has softened his view of Butt.

"Well, you couldn't have said anything better," John replies with a genuine grin. This must be his birthday present. The fates have remembered to give him a gift.

Upstairs in a private room at the Lord Nelson, Dr. Butt and Dr. Young talk over issues with four rabbis, two from New York and two from Nova Scotia, and a few prominent Jewish businessmen from Halifax.

John starts them off. "I am aware of the issues with autopsies and your faith, but now you see why we must conduct examinations and use whatever means possible to identify the remains."

Rabbi Krupka takes up the conversation. "We are concerned with means of identification. However, it's a more complex issue than you may understand."

John and James listen intently while Rabbi Krupka explains the need for a vital part of the body. "If all you find is the bone from an ankle, then we can't sit shiva and the widow can never remarry."

"I don't know if we can promise to identify something vital for all of the Jewish passengers. I have no idea what we'll recover in the end."

"We have an identification expert in Israel who deals with all these unpleasant things, like explosions, and puts a stamp on the identification to say this person is dead. That's our tradition, and it's our rule. So we'd like to bring this expert over to authenticate the deaths. Would you be willing to have him here?"

John gets the impression that the local rabbis are a little miffed that the Americans are stepping in, suggesting they don't have the ability to look after the victims' needs. But Rabbi Krupka has presented a problem and a solution, ready to go, and no one else seems to be piping up with other ideas.

"No question about it." The relief of shedding this problem is immediate. "Done," John says, with a snap of his fingers. "Consider it done." Of course he knows the RCMP aren't going to like it, but that's their problem. Decisions about the identification and handling of the remains are entirely under his authority. He is more than happy to get this issue resolved in such an affable manner. His relationship with these cops is all shot to hell anyway. They are too officious in the face of this madness, and their rigid application of the rules is really getting on his nerves. It is easier and easier to say yes to the families and no to the RCMP. John plans to champion the remains until every person on that plane is identified and put to rest.

"You're a mensch, Dr. Butt." With that, the anxiously anticipated meeting is over.

John and James go to a restaurant in Dartmouth for birthday dinner and drinks. By John's standards, the place is a dump. But it doesn't matter much. His team gave him a cake, his "Rabbi Gluck" trouble is a thing of the past, and he doesn't have to stand on that stage at the Lord Nelson again. He feels good. *This hasn't been such a bad birthday after all.*

That night, back in the barracks at Shearwater, John finally gets some sleep.

CHAPTER ELEVEN

THINGS FALL APART

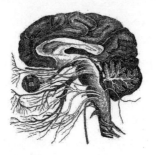

IN THE BACK of a cab, on a frigid winter night in Calgary, John re-ignited his long-suppressed and carefully concealed desires. He'd been out for dinner with his wife and friends. They'd carpooled to the restaurant in John's new green Volvo, and were left stranded later when the engine resolutely refused to turn over in the spanking Alberta cold. The women were sent home in a cab while the men waited for a tow truck. Once their duty was done, they climbed into a cab of their own.

They'd been drinking. They were gregarious, even flirtatious, rolling along in the dark backseat. John made a pass. It was a spontaneous act, motivated by the moment and the inebriants. He was not rebuked, as he had been in his teen years with other boys. The two married men kissed passionately. Flashes of the sparkling, snowy landscape, illuminated by the street lamps they sped past, decorated the night's exhilarating ride.

It was 1977. Four provinces and thousands of kilometres away, Quebec had signalled a new era in Canadian law by including sexual orientation in the Human Rights Code. It became illegal to discriminate based on one's preference of partner. Employers, landlords, and hoteliers throughout the French-Canadian province were no longer able to fire gay employees for being gay, or refuse service to same-sex couples. The Albertans, with their cowboy hats and gold-star hearts, shook their heads and averted their eyes. They were rugged. They knew blood, dirt, and money. They were men who did not tolerate sissies.

John and his friend didn't rejoin their wives immediately. They took a detour in the taxi and stopped by the friend's home to continue their fun while the women waited at the Butt family home. It signalled the beginning of a change for John, though he didn't realize it at the time.

Earlier that fall, Barb had suggested it was time to split up. John refused to hear her, yet again. The idea terrified him, and he tried to insist it away. Then, his close friend, a buddy since childhood, had John over to watch a football game and share a bit of dinner. Between downs, the men struggled through a difficult conversation.

"My marriage is over, John," his friend confessed.

"I'm sorry to hear that."

"You know our wives have been talking a lot, don't you?"

His friend's wife had spent a good deal of time sitting up late with Barb in the kitchen after John had gone to bed. But Barb was a talker, so John thought nothing of it.

"Well, they're talking about you. And it doesn't sound good."

John sputtered a little, bristling at the subject he worked so hard to keep at bay.

"Look," his buddy said, "your marriage is on the rocks. Barb is going to leave you. There's nothing you can do about it. It's time to accept what's really going on here."

John refused to get into it, and quickly steered the conversation back to his friend's failed marriage. He didn't want to think about divorce. It was shameful. Embarrassing. Low-class. He intended to keep his family together, despite the cold war he'd been fighting with his wife for years.

By the summer of 1978, with John still living in his house of cards, Barb took the girls and the Volvo station wagon to her family's summer cabin on the west coast, and John stayed behind to work. While they were gone, he had the carpets replaced as an insistent display of ownership. The installers knocked a pile of Barb's papers from the phone alcove and left them scattered on the floor. John flipped through a spiral bound notebook. It was, essentially, filled with the details of her divorce plan. He felt the panic rise. He didn't want to be a divorcée. He'd worked so hard to be admired in the community and he wanted success, not stigma.

The panic took over as he leafed through the lists and legal notes in Barb's book. Acceptance of this reality before him was nowhere to be found. Instead, he hatched a plan. What he needed was a grand gesture. He went to a Toyota dealership and bought a new sporty Celica for Barb, then packed up the dog and drove the car over the mountains for the big reveal.

"Come look, I've bought you a new car!" he announced upon his arrival at his in-law's summer cottage.

Barb didn't appear interested in the gift. As always, and despite his late efforts, she remained a sealed story to him. The vacation was another silent retreat for the long-suffering pair, and John fumed while Barb ignored him. The tandem convoy home with two kids and the dog didn't improve matters. Barb, in her new sporty car, was pulled over by the police, while John, who was ahead in the Volvo, sped away unfettered.

In September, after the Butt family returned from their island holiday, John tried to continue on as if everything were fine. When the monthly bills came, he was floored by a $500 tally for one month of spending at the Hudson's Bay. Barb had been shopping, a lot. He flashed back to the notebook with the divorce plan and assumed this was her stockpiling, preparing for the split. On Saturday, he went around to all of the major department stores and closed Barb's credit card accounts. After informing his wife of her new credit-less status, he went out for an evening on the town without her. When he got home, she'd locked him out. He broke in through a flimsy screen door, clomped into the bedroom, and slept beside his stiffened wife. Denial was easier than the alternative.

John went back to work on Monday, roughed-up, but still maintaining control, so he thought. The receptionist called him to the front. Someone with a name John didn't recognize insisted he speak with Dr. Butt face to face. He strode out of his office, ready to assume his role as the man in charge, and deal with whomever and whatever. At least he knew how to handle work problems efficiently. But it wasn't about work. A man handed John a manila envelope from a family law office. He was being served. Barb had filed for a legal separation. The documents stipulated John was to be out of their family home within a month. Finally, after fourteen years of struggle, denial lost out.

On Saturday, October 17, 1978, John moved out of his family home and into an apartment near the Foothills Hospital. He furnished his living room with lawn furniture and his kitchen with the few items he'd taken from home. At that time in the evolution of divorce, the children and the house stayed with the wife, almost by default. Barb called him a few days after he'd moved, "You've taken my double boiler, and I'd like it back."

Fuck you and your double boiler, he thought, shifting uncomfortably in his skeletal lawn chair. He felt broke. He had no furniture, no yard, and no family. Over half his salary was going to support Barb and the girls, and pay the mortgage on a house he didn't live in. It felt like failure.

The split brought new freedom, but he was reluctant to explore it. Dinner parties populated with handsome men became part of his social life. Despite the titillation, he wasn't stimulated by the conversations. He didn't feel compelled to expand his time with Calgary's hidden homosexual cohort. They liked to travel en masse to Puerto Vallarta and stay at all-inclusive, gay-friendly resorts. It sounded hideous to John. The dinner parties were fun, but the lifestyle wasn't a fit for his vision of himself. He certainly couldn't show up to the annual Naval Ball or an Alberta Justice affair with a guy on his arm. An established and mature man in the community arriving stag at a social function wasn't appropriate either, unless he was a widower. John needed a socialite lady for such occasions, and it didn't take him long to find one.

On April Fool's Day, John went for a romantic dinner at an

Italian restaurant with Mary. They'd met at a social function a few years earlier, and he asked her out when they met again at a mutual friend's house more recently. Mary, tall and elegant, was a divorcée with daughters close to the age of John's girls. After scampi and wine, John made his intentions clear in a properly vague way. "Do you want to go home?"

At John's place in the south tower by the hospital, they became a twosome. They went on camping trips with the kids, cooked dinners together, and explored the countryside on long drives. They went to fancy parties and decadent galas. Society was important. Mary wore long, slender gowns and elbow-length white gloves, her arm linked in John's, standing as her erect escort in his Navy dress uniform with gold braid and white officer's hat. They danced, dined, and rumpled the sheets while his wife twisted the financial screws from the house across town.

Serving as Alberta's first Chief Medical Examiner was presenting its own challenges. John had grown up in Alberta, and felt he knew the place well. Then, a First Nations Cree community in Northern Alberta brought baseball bats to welcome a small plane filled with RCMP officers sent to retrieve remains for examination. Suspicious deaths on Reserve required investigation under the criminal code, including an autopsy of the body. But the Cree people had specific rituals around death and the handling of corpses. The RCMP violated the dead by removing them from the community and treating them without appropriate respect. The situation had come to a head, and John's boss, the Deputy Minister, insisted it was time for Alberta's freshly minted Chief Medical Examiner to step in and smooth things over. Perhaps, with a proper explanation from the right authority, the Cree people might be more cooperative.

John prepared an informative presentation and took a small, chartered plane from High Level to Garden River, near the border between Alberta and the Northwest Territories. He was nervous. This entire scenario was new. He had little experience with First Nations people. In the seventies, though not an official policy, segregation was the norm in Alberta. His detailed medical education provided little to no psychology or sociology content. Medical mysteries were his medium of choice.

At the longhouse meeting, John waited for his turn to address the crowd with his presentation designed to guide them through the process of death investigation. It didn't work that way. There were no speeches, as such. Everyone spoke. It was a giant conversation between many people that went on and on. Unwritten rules, to which John was oblivious, kept the speakers in check, but still allowed everyone to be heard. The doctor sat and waited to be called upon, despite his evaporating patience.

After more than an hour, a man finally addressed the Chief Medical Examiner. "Doctor, when you are in the morgue and you move the body, are you marching slowly?"

What the fuck are you talking about? John thought. "No," was what he managed to say out loud.

Dr. Butt was there to talk about law, and truth, and the importance of those things, not silly funerary stuff. The community was focused on the stewardship of souls in his care, but the language wasn't in John's wheelhouse at the time. He found the discussion ridiculous.

The meeting went on and on, but appeared to solve nothing. By the time he arrived home, exhausted, the trip seemed a waste. The government spent tax dollars to send him up there on a chartered plane, and he'd fretted over the affair and prepared things to say, then hardly delivered any of it. *What difference did that make?*

There was no doubt, death investigation came with grieving people. But at the time, John didn't see his job as dealing with them directly. One of his greatest successes was the introduction of Nurse Medical Investigators. The idea had been brewing in his mind ever since he did his tour of American ME facilities on his way home from Europe. In New York City, a driver was dispatched to fetch the duty doctor when a call came in. Every scene had a set of medical eyes along with police eyes. John felt it gave them a good investigative start, with the bounty of expertise ensuring no evidence was overlooked.

Dr. Butt preferred nurses who'd had emergency or intensive care experience. Once, he'd hired a paramedic, but had to fire him. During the investigation of a suicide, complete with good-bye note, the young man couldn't bring himself to rule it as such. John had to step in and put the matter to rest, signing off on the cause of death. A straightforward suicide is not reason enough for a full-on investigation, or existential crisis. The Nurse Investigators were the ME's first responders, and they had to decide on a course of action based on their findings at any death scene. John found the ER nurses had a no nonsense approach that fit the role perfectly.

* * *

Pat Bruni started as a Nurse Investigator with the Calgary Office of the Chief Medical Examiner in 1982. She was young and fun: curvy and compact with a pile of black hair and chocolate eyes. She loved to laugh, and had a genuine desire to connect with people. She'd moved from Ontario to follow her boyfriend and she wanted a break from the emergency room. Nurse Bruni had struggled with grieving families when patients died. She didn't know what to do with her own feelings. A death scene investigator role offered a chance to meet that challenge head on. That was Pat's style.

Bruni met the Chief ME on her first day at the office in early August of '82. When the supervisor introduced them, Dr. Butt was preoccupied and the meeting was brief, but he managed to fit in a witty comment, perhaps something he kept up his sleeve to welcome the newbies and give them a sense of the atmosphere. *Oh my gawd,* Bruni thought to herself as she laughed, head thrown back, *he's funny!* She'd worked with her share of over-bearing doctors with zero people skills and was excited to see her new boss showing his humanity straight away. He put her at ease.

Pat spent two months studying the law, riding along with other investigators, learning Dr. Butt's specific investigation methods, and memorizing what to look for in particular situations. Her first solo death scene investigation was on a sunny fall day around nine in the morning.

A call came from Emergency Medical Services. "We have a baby death in southwest Calgary ..."

Pat scribbled the address and relevant info in her notebook, called the body removal service to schedule a pick up, and headed to the retired ghost car used by the ME office for investigations. It's important to get there as quickly as possible to preserve the scene. A child is easy to pick up and move around. Her nerves jangled all the way to the site. Two police cars and an ambulance with lights flashing crowded the front of the bungalow, noses pointing toward the door like bloodhounds.

A baby death was particular. Dr. Butt had underlined a handful of scenes that needed specific inspection, and specific questions answered. This was one of those scenes. Pat wanted more than anything to do this right, to look professional in front of the police, and to get answers to every question her boss might ask at the review. Butt was a stickler for detail.

OK, here we go, she thought, heading up the front walk. An officer met her at the door. The distraught parents sat on the living room couch, clinging to one another. Two more officers pointed the way to the baby's room, and followed her down the hall. There was a rocking chair, a padded change table, and a crib with a mobile of colourful fish dangling from above. The room was tidy and smelled clean.

Pat walked to the crib. The child looked normal, three to four months old, wrapped in a blanket that the paramedics had pulled down, along with the baby's sleeper, in their attempts to revive the child. She touched the body. It was cold and stiff, already in rigor. There were no toys in the crib and she found no signs of blood or bruising anywhere on the body. Two men from the removal service arrived.

"I want just one of you to carry this child out in the blanket, but wait until I've finished with the parents," Pat told them. She felt elbow-to-elbow in the small room with four men when she realized the distraught mother was the only other woman around.

Pat went out to the living room and introduced herself to the parents after she had connected with the body and noted the scene. The father was angry. He held his weeping wife, trying in vain to protect her from the tragedy. A small gang of police lingered in the room. Pat asked them to step outside so she could have a private talk with the family. The tension eased a little at their departure. She was a nurse after all, a woman without a gun, without suspicion, just here to talk.

Pat sat on the overstuffed chair adjacent to the couch with her notebook open on her lap. She asked a litany of probing, sometimes personal questions in a soft but professional tone. How was the pregnancy? Were there complications? Birth weight? Breast or formula, which kind, how often, how much, last time? She asked whether or not they had any family history of diabetes, or hypertension, if they smoke, drink, or use illicit drugs. The father was very abrupt, to the point of abrasive, when she asked him about his family history. That threw Pat off, but she kept at it. In her head, she tried desperately to remember all of what John Butt told her to find out.

When Pat stood to leave, the mother became distraught again. The young nurse investigator wanted to know what to say, what to do. She took this job to develop a dialect around grief, and here was her first test.

"Do you want to hold the baby?" she asked the mother.

"Enough!" the father said.

As the police blocked the parents' view to the front door, a man they didn't know carried their child's body away. Pat stayed facing the parents. She wanted to give them any solace she could. At this point, the body was all she had to offer.

"You can still come to the office and hold the child if you want. But we will have to do an autopsy." She handed her card to the inconsolable mother.

After the autopsy, Pat had to call the family. "Unfortunately, we have no definitive results on the cause of death for you, but the baby's body can be released." She felt the importance of the remains, both to the ME's investigation, and to the loved ones.

But the extensive testing had yielded nothing of note to indicate manner or cause of death, and therefore, was ruled another instance of Sudden Infant Death Syndrome.

Death in the ME office was the beginning of a mystery, unlike a hospital death signalling the end of a search for solutions. It required a different mindset. Sometimes, mysteries were unsolvable, and those were perhaps the hardest cases to put to rest.

* * *

On Nov 26, 1982, Judge Brennan of Alberta Queen's Bench ruled on the divorce proceedings of *Butt v. Butt* after a lengthy battle over money. John didn't contest his wife's petition for custody of the kids. Women and children belonged together. In the four years of separation, Barb had continued to live in the family home with the kids, and completed a bachelor degree in nursing. John's salary financed everything. She wanted to continue on to law school. Barb filed an action pursuant to the fairly new *Matrimonial Property Act* (1980), hoping the court would rule in favour of John continuing to pay the mortgage, support her, the children, and pay for her legal education after the divorce. She had, after all, provided support for John when he was studying abroad.

The judge didn't see things entirely her way. She was suing John for divorce based on cruelty. Brennan ruled in her favour there, but he didn't agree with John paying for more education in another field when she was already qualified to work. She could stay in the house and John had to pay her alimony and support for the kids, but he was no longer required to pay for her further education, or the mortgage on the house. Barb, despite the blow, followed through on her plan, finishing law school while raising the girls and working. When the marriage officially ended, Jessica and Kimberly were teenagers.

In 1983, the Office of the Chief Medical Examiner's state-of-the-art facility in Calgary was completed. A matching building in Edmonton had been completed in 1981. The square brick buildings were early '80s tributes to mid-century modern architecture. The Calgary facility was tucked in a hollow on the side of a hill, close to the University of Calgary. Inside the double glass doors, tall green-ery, a fountain, and several semi-secluded benches formed an open square solarium in the center of the building, with a large reception desk off to one side. The offices were arranged around the perimeter, with the autopsy suite in the corner, and a loading bay around back. Both buildings were fully equipped, each with its own histology and toxicology lab, and all the specialized, expensive medical machin-ery required.

By the mid eighties, with the Office of the Chief ME well in hand, John took control of his personal life again. He'd purchased a lot with a view and oversaw the construction of his dream home. He moved to his new place at the end of 1984, and Kimberly, his younger daughter, moved in with him. His ex-wife and older daugh-ter were relocating to Vancouver, and the girls didn't want their dad to be alone, so Kim decided to stay. She was very athletic, and en-couraged John to get in shape. The pair went running together and he joined a volleyball league at the hospital. He didn't care that most of the players were at least ten years younger. Before long, he'd lost 50 pounds and was as fit as he'd ever been.

He and Mary were still having a wonderful time together, and his girls loved her.

John liked to show off a bit for Mary. He kept a stash of body tags in the glove compartment of his car. When they pulled up next to a motorcycle at a stoplight, John asked Mary to pass him a body tag. He rolled down his window with the electric control on his armrest and passed the tag to the rider.

"You'll need it soon."

He loved the look on the young guy's face. John and Mary laughed, secure in their steel cage wrapped in metal. He thought he'd finally triumphed. He was at the forefront of his profession, had a lady friend who adored him, a house he designed, and at least one of his daughters to round out the image of a family. He was fit and full of life at age 50.

John attended a large birthday party for a friend's mid-life mile-stone. Mary wasn't with him that night. These were old friends and catching up would keep him busy. John stood in the middle of the sunken living room, cocktail in hand, regaling the guys with some gruesome tale or other, when Alex appeared at the top of the stairs. It had been at least twenty years since he last saw his beloved friend. Alex and John had spent many happy days together as pubescent boys, but they lost touch when John went off to a different high school. The last time he'd seen Alex, his boyhood friend had been standing buck naked in the University men's room showers, toweling himself off. John had stared, startled by the beauty of the young man's athletic figure. Alex had tried to act casual, as if nothing had ever happened between them. Maybe that's the way Alex thought about their adolescent love affair. Or maybe he didn't think of it at all.

Holy Christ, John whispered to himself, as he watched Alex descend the stairs and move through the crowd of guests at the birthday party. His heart pounded in his chest. They said hello and had a brief, superficial chat before Alex moved on to other conversations. John didn't believe his own reaction. He felt flustered and weak-kneed. His palms sweated and his face flushed. *What was it about this guy that shook him up so much? Why the visceral reaction?* When the party was over, John gathered up the pieces of his unrequited crush, stuffed them back inside, and tried to shove them down.

It didn't work.

CHAPTER TWELVE

MEMORIAL

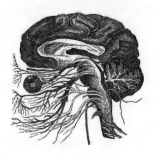

DR. BUTT STANDS in one of the thirteen refrigerated semi trailers parked behind Hangar B at Shearwater. Hundreds of bagged and tagged body parts line the metal shelves running the length of the fifty-three-foot metal box. Plastic tubs bearing names of victims hold pieces of identified remains. Other bins hold unidentified remains, yet to be processed. None of these victims will be whole again. Eventually, enough flesh and bone will be identified to confirm exactly who had been on that plane. The Nova Scotia Government's duty to the victims will be done. Months from now, when the search is finally over, thousands of pieces of humanity will sit side-by-side in darkened freezers, waiting for a final resting place.

When John left the Lord Nelson Hotel that first, definitive Friday night, he was soaked through with heavy emotion. In the ballroom full of grief-stricken families, John had found a new piece of himself. Usually, the victims' loved ones stay on one side of death with the anguish, while he stands on the other side with law, science, and a job to do. Not this time.

Six days in and John has done so many interviews with the media he's become the face of the tragedy. People are remarking on his emotional state. "It's obvious that it's beginning to take its toll," the news anchor Peter Mansbridge says as John struggles to get through his answers during an interview for the nightly news.

* * *

During a panel discussion on the national news, Mark Herbert sees Dr. Butt on screen, pale as a ghost, answering one difficult question after another with a cracking voice. Mark has been trying to call John for days. When he sees his friend struggling on television or hears the ME's wavering voice on the radio, tears come to his eyes.

Mark is young, fit, and handsome. He's also John's image of a perfect man, or son. They met through John's younger daughter, Kimberly, when Mark was 24. Kim and Mark had a fling at a Club Med where she worked as a fitness instructor and Mark was a guest on vacation. Kim told Mark he'd probably get on gangbusters with her dad. They shared the same sense of humour.

The men have been friends for more than ten years now. Mark knows how badly John needs a shoulder, so he keeps calling. "John! I finally got hold of you. You're all over the news."

"It's bloody awful, Mark, just bloody awful. There are no bodies. No bodies!"

Mark wishes he wasn't so far away. "I have to come see you. When can I visit?"

"I haven't been home since the crash. I don't know when it will end." John is under great strain, but he's in his element. This is the dichotomy of Mark's dear friend; for John, satisfaction comes at great peril.

* * *

Shearwater is the intake center for every physical piece of what remains. Handfuls of American one hundred dollar bills recovered from the scene dry in makeshift huts attached to industrial blowers and heaters behind the mortuary. The freshly minted money had been in the cargo hold, bound for Geneva. RCMP officers hold the only key to the cash hut. They log every bill before placing it on one of many wire shelves and locking it up.

A decontamination shower is constructed on the dock at Shearwater for the workers returning from search sessions covered in remnants of viscera. Water and fuel-logged seat cushions are pressed flat by a giant wringer mechanism on shore. Victims' personal effects are also sent through the dryer huts, then laid on tables in a long tent beside the hangar for identification. All of these necessary pieces of the operation are cobbled together, their needfulness unknown until the problems arise.

Ron Jeppesen, the lead construction man on site, is faced with new building challenges every day. The current pressing issue is the smell. Decomp is in full swing at Hangar B. Workers arrive in the morning, smear camphor ointment under their nostrils, then don paper masks in an effort to avoid the overwhelming stench. Ron and his team construct an elaborate industrial exhaust system over the morgue and X-ray areas. The thrumming fans pull the air up and away. There is an improvement, but the machine is no match for Mother Nature's scent mechanisms, designed to attract the appropriate attendants of death. The overpowering smell is omnipresent despite Ron's team and all of their ingenuity.

After an hour in the paper mask, Ron pulls it off, annoyed. It gets in the way of his vision when he works. But he's used to the smell now. Cadaverine and putrescine molecules have bonded with the scent receptors in his olfactory bulbs, numbing him to further intense sensation. He's getting used to a lot of things here. As he climbs up and down, gearing overhead fixtures, he pays no mind to the young woman's body lying on the striker table next to him. The figure has no legs, only one arm, and half of a head. There's no blood. Like all of the other remains, the body is clean from the water of St. Margaret's Bay. Some of the guys have quit, and he doesn't blame them. The bodies may not be a problem for Ron, but when he's working over at Hangar A, where all of the non-biological remains are processed, the sight of a shredded teddy bear almost breaks him.

He drives home after a decontamination shower on the dock, thinking he's left the smell evidence behind. But the next morning, when he opens the car door, the air tracked home from the morgue trounces him once again.

* * *

On Tuesday, September 8th, six days post-crash, *USS Grapple* arrives with a crane capable of lifting 300 tons. A crew of highly trained divers uses the vessel as a base. A remote operating vehicle, or ROV, is sent to the ocean floor to scout for remains of the aircraft and passengers. Once a report is sent back, the divers go down and attach lines or gather body parts in bags and send them to the surface in a net. Divers travel with their own psychiatrist but the regular sailors are unprepared for what lies beneath them.

John likes to tour the vessels involved in the recovery operation at least once. Since the first request from Commander Town the morning after the crash, John feels a sense of duty to the tireless and dedicated Navy crews. Some of them are obviously inexperienced. He can't imagine facing this carnage straight out of training.

On the deck of *USS Grapple*, a young woman in uniform leans over a mess of net and body bags. John watches her from a few feet away. He can feel her anguish as she picks at something tangled in the net.

"What have you got there?" he asks, peering over her shoulder.

"I don't even know, Sir."

It's a small piece of human fat. Beyond that, there is nothing recognizable about it. It may never be identified, yet it still needs a number, a log entry, a photograph, a bag, and a documented place in one of the refrigerated trucks back at the morgue.

"Do you have any understanding of why you're doing this?" he asks her.

"No." The single word expresses a world of confusion.

"This is a hard job, but it's not just a job. There's no question about it, this is not just a job."

"Sir?"

"You know the families of these victims will never see their loved ones again? You represent those families here. Your care is their comfort." John tries to hold her up with his earnest expressions. He wants her to know she is valuable. Her bravery spurs him on, and he traverses the ship's decks, giving encouragement where he can.

Once back at the morgue, the inspiration from the selfless workers on the ship dissolves into annoyance. The Jewish doctor, sent by Rabbi Krupka, seems to have little interest in anything like work. He made a great show of touring the facility and nodding approval at the set-up. Since then, as far as John can tell, he sits around eating the local ladies' baked goodies, if he's around at all. And Dr. Young's usefulness is tempered by the Coroner's desire for attention, as John sees it.

"I've had a call from my journalist friend at the *Toronto Star*," Young tells Butt after the morning meeting.

Here it comes, John thinks.

"I've got a very good rapport with her and I'd like to do a telephone interview," Young says.

John is already annoyed with Young for walking around with a camera on his neck, snapping photos of this and that in the morgue. Other than the official police and ME documentation teams, no one has a camera in the morgue. John let it slide at first because Young was helpful and they had important work to do. But now the Coroner wants to get in front of the media, and that won't do. The Chief ME works with the press officer for the Attorney General's Office. She guides him with an expert hand, telling him what not to do, and what needs to be said. He feels safe in her hands with their well-crafted message for public consumption. But John has no control over Young, and no idea what he'll say or do.

"No." the ME's response is short and succinct, delivered in a tone that discourages further discussion.

Wednesday, September 9th, marks one-week post tragedy. A memorial at a school in Indian Harbour, on the field under a marquee, starts in the late afternoon. It's a glorious, sunny fall day; the opposite of last Wednesday's cold rain and low clouds. The Prime Minister of Canada, Jean Chrétien, flies in for the event, and wants to meet Nova Scotia's Chief Medical Examiner. At 3 p.m., John is driven to the airport in time for the PM's arrival. The men shake hands but say little.

When the entourage of leaders leaves the airport, John rides in a military van with two senior officers, but no Navy men. The route takes the cavalcade down a long stretch of highway, to the turn off at Upper Tantallon, the same exit John uses to get home from work. Home. The dogs. It seems so far away.

He's glad to be in the back, alone, as they wind south along Route 333, rolling over one whale's back hump of granite after another. The landscape dips and rises outside the window. It's rocky and scrubby green with patches of luscious vegetation where little houses gather around whitewashed churches and graveyards of tilted headstones. They whiz by a house and a streak of colour catches John's eye, then another and another. Yellow ribbons tie flowers to fence posts and mail boxes. Hand-painted signs accompany the bouquets. He scans them as they pass. *Our Hearts Are With You. We Are Thinking of You.* John has a new appreciation for the people of Nova Scotia. Their response to this horrible event is stupendous. The sentiments bring on more tears. He's constantly steeling himself against the emotional tsunami of situations, but the triggers are everywhere, flooding his defenses, catching him off guard.

* * *

Here it is time for the first memorial and Linda still doesn't know how she's getting to the service. The RCMP are saying nobody's allowed to take their car to the school where it's happening. Dr. Butt's gone off with the bigwigs, so there's no riding with him. Apparently, there are designated parking lots, and then, supposedly, shuttles to the school. She borrows her husband's new, black Mustang with fat, gold stripes, and follows the directions to a parking lot.

Linda stands and waits for a shuttle. Car after car drives by.

People wave. Everyone can see her standing there in her smart orange blazer. There goes the mayor. No one stops to park or fetch her. *Where do they think they're going?* She's going to be late. Finally, a sedan slows and pulls into the parking lot.

"Excuse me," the driver says.

Linda leans into the window after he calls her over.

"They should have a parking attendant at every lot. Everywhere else is all jumbled and I don't know how anybody is going to get out. You're doing a wonderful job here." Then he drives away.

Linda is so exasperated, all she can do is laugh. *Everyone thinks I'm a parking attendant!*

She doesn't make it to the one-week memorial. She stands on side of the road next to her parked car waiting to be picked up until after the ceremony has started. Images of Dr. Butt sitting up there, knowing her seat is empty and not doing anything about it, convince her to get back in the Mustang and hit the road toward home. There's no way she's going up there now, late and alone.

* * *

The service is populated with local broken hearts. Fishermen who walked the shoreline or scanned the water sit here. Women who baked endless cakes and made mountains of sandwiches to feed the work-effort sit here. Service men and women from all arms of protection forces sit together on the field at an elementary school in a small harbour town trying to find their way back to the home they knew.

The ceremony starts with a Mi'kmaq drummer, beating rhythm while she performs a traditional prayer. She describes the circle of life. Another local woman stands and enunciates the name of each of the 229 victims of Swissair Flight 111. Her eastern Canadian accent folds roughly over foreign sounds, but her heartache resonates with each syllable. A string of religious men take turns with their sermons, each offering solace in his own way.

Bob Conrad is at the memorial ceremony, too. He's impressed with the spiritual leaders who seem to be supporting one another without prejudice. As a devout Seventh Day Adventist with a degree in religious studies, Bob knows the lines between religious affiliations have been drawn with a priori epistemology. He's never seen a priest minister alongside a pastor and a rabbi. It's an odd thing to be here, on the elementary school field, under a tent top, listening to this disparate collection of prayers and sermons. But it's working. It's beautiful.

This bay is a roughly hewn horseshoe basin of Atlantic Ocean, fringed with granite boulders, sandy beaches, tiny fishing villages, and the occasional exquisite home. Postcard scenery abounds. Residents fear what they may find in the craggy spaces of their beloved seashore. *Will it ever be the same again?* Bob wonders. No one wants to eat the seafood caught in or near the bay. Even if they did, Bob's fishing spots, along with the territories of many other tuna fishermen, have been shut down for the duration of the investigation. No one has any idea how long that will be. The fishermen are missing the most lucrative season, but it's not what weighs on him the most. Everyday activities aren't working right. His mind seems less capable and he worries how Peggy, his wife, is dealing with these new, raw parts of him.

* * *

Back at Shearwater the next day, Linda flips through a growing stack of unofficial correspondence. The envelopes are cream, even soft pink, with hand-written addresses in looped and slanted script. Here's another distraction. Dr. Butt is all over the TV and in the papers. He's gone and made himself the tissue for everyone's tears and now he's going to drown. But what can she do about it? She's not playing babysitter. Linda takes the pile of stationery and drops it on Dr. Butt's desk.

"What happened to you yesterday?" he asks.

"I stood on the side of the road waiting for a ride and everybody drove right by me! And you're sitting up there next to an empty seat? Where did you think I was?"

These are rhetorical questions, John knows. Linda makes an abrupt turn and stomps out of the office. They both know there's no point discussing the matter further. *How the hell was I supposed to know she needed a ride?* he thinks.

John regards the pile of letters with some trepidation. They've been arriving in mounds since the weekend. People pour out their grief or give their hearts for what they imagine John is enduring. And for the most part, they've got it right. But their words, while often uplifting, keep his emotions at the surface. Letters from other healthcare workers tell him what a great thing he is doing for the profession; letters from families thank him for the compassion and engagement; old friends in the medical profession send him a pat on the back and a stiff upper lip; strangers from St. Margaret's Bay shake his hand with their words.

One local lady writes: "I'm sure you know how proud your father would be of you ..." Another offers: "When you feel up to it, my butterfly leg of lamb awaits ..."

The president of an Albertan memorial service provider says: "I know there isn't a medical examiner in the country that is more capable of getting this difficult task completed than you are, John."

Many of the missives refer to recent newspaper or television reports featuring John and his newly exposed, emotional self. Everyone is thinking of him and praising him for his compassion. The spotlight continues to catch him off-guard for the entire world to see.

Chapter Thirteen

DISASTER TRAINING

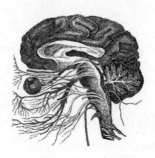

"Do you know there's been a bad rail crash west of Edmonton?" Pat Bruni, the investigator from John's Calgary office, was on the phone. It was late on a Saturday afternoon.

"No, I don't know anything about it." John was a bit confused. If there'd been a major accident, his Deputy Chief in the Edmonton office, Dr. Derrick Pounder, should have called him straight away.

"It's been on the news. I wanted to be sure you knew." By the time Pat called, the crash was already eight hours old.

On Saturday, February 8th, 1986, at 8:40 on a cold Alberta morning near the town of Hinton, west of Edmonton, a west-bound Canadian National Railway freight train collided head on with an east-bound Via Rail passenger train. The freight train failed to slow or stop according to the signal lights. When it blew through the red over red, the train was travelling at close to 100 kilometres per hour, well over the limit on that stretch of track.

The chain of freight cars collided with the oncoming Via Rail train and plowed over the passenger cars. The engines, each pulling a line of linked vessels loaded with cargo or people, were destroyed on impact. Iron tubes loaded with grain and steel boxes full of sulphur buckled at their connections, twisting perpendicular to the track

and pooling around the site of impact. Diesel bled from the loco-
motives and caught fire, engulfing several cars. Bright orange tongues
licked the winter sky, defiant against the snow-covered landscape.

A coach car and glass-domed café car were crushed. Punctured
freight cars poured their contents through the smashed-in roofs,
submerging the fatalities and wounded in a dry quicksand of ker-
nels. Wheat rolled down the embankment beside the tracks and
turned winter white to summer-straw yellow. Emergency responders
sprayed truckloads of water over the heart of the collision. As the
flames died, the water seeped down beneath the grain and turned to
a sheet of ice. At mid-day, with rescue and recovery in full swing,
the thermostat read minus thirteen degrees Celsius.

Dr. Derrick Pounder, a young Welshman who had come to
Canada after a stint in Australia, earned his forensic pathology credentials in Dublin, Ireland. Several men had held the Deputy Chief
ME position since Dr. Markesteyn left a decade earlier. John had
trouble finding a forensic pathologist who was willing to play second
fiddle in his orchestra. Dr. Pounder wasn't faring any better than his
predecessors. When Hinton happened, Derrick didn't call the Chief
ME. He went straight to the scene and took over. He conducted
press conferences and barked at RCMP officers while Dr. Butt was
none the wiser.

John was furious. He was the one who had to talk to the Minister.
What if his boss had called for details and he was caught knowing
nothing? Derrick had overstepped, again. The Edmonton office
could have some autonomy, but this was ridiculous. Within hours of
the call, John was on a government plane flying north with Nurse
Investigator Pat Bruni at his side.

The accident scene was treacherous. Twisted metal and rolling
grain over a layer of invisible ice made for a dangerous site. By the
time John arrived, there were dozens of RCMP members working
with the Transportation Safety Board, documenting and guarding
the scene. Dr. Butt did his best to ignore Pounder while he assessed
the situation. So long as things were running smoothly, John wasn't

going to make a fuss, for now. After his survey of the crash site, the Chief ME headed back to Edmonton to handle the political side of this disaster.

⁓ They set up a command post at the northern office. John spoke to the Minister and Deputy, informing everyone of the situation. He didn't know how many were dead at the time, but he saw the wreckage. It was worse than the Hither Green disaster years ago with Professor Simpson. He saw the potential for mass fatality in the heaped up train cars and wafting smoke. He knew what was coming.

* * *

Pat Bruni was teamed up with six RCMP officers. Their job was to clear the coach car where most of the fatalities occurred. First they had to get to it. A sea of grain three and four feet deep surrounded the impact site, and the coach sat under a stack of freight cars. The work was grueling. Moving was difficult. A massive crane was employed to lift the railcars. Emergency workers cut through mangled metal with power tools. Sparks and diesel filled the air. A square foot-by-foot grid strategy was used to document everything. The human remains were mostly bones, though one nearly intact body was found in the locomotive's toilet, and a partial body was removed from within the wheel trucks. But the fire incinerated the flesh of most remains, and continued to smoulder under the grain, burning away the victims' identities. Pat found the skull of an engineer in the grain outside the locomotive. She assumed the victim had been decapitated. The damage was tremendous.

Pat was one of very few women working on site, inside and around the wreckage. Everyone was dressed in white, one-piece snowsuits outside, with their hoods up to guard against the negative temperature. Gender was hidden under the mounds of insulation. When she pushed her hood down, picking up lunch at the dining trailer for the first time, and exposed her pretty face and long dark hair, many of the railway men did not approve.

"This is no place for a woman," they said.

Pat smiled and kept walking. She knew her gender often offered a window of connection with the grief-stricken that helped her in her work. She knew she was in the right place. At least her team of RCMP guys treated her well, even though they teased the crap out of her. The guys thought it was fun to toss her out the window into the grain and watch her swim back, then struggle to get in. And they loved it when she accidentally left her camera next to the propane heater. It melted until nothing was left but the lens. She'd never lived that down. Humour was a key element to surviving this work and the emotionally charged environment. Her job was always a challenge, and just the way she liked it.

* * *

By Tuesday, four days in, the tension was rising. The weather remained frigid, the site was no less treacherous, and tempers were growing hot. John flew back and forth between the information command center in Edmonton and the scene of the crash.

"Doc, I need to talk to you," an RCMP sergeant said to the Chief ME at the Edmonton office. "We really can't work with Dr. Pounder anymore."

"Why? What's happened?"

"The guys are working hard out there, and it's pretty dangerous, what we're doing. It's important we all get along, or somebody could get hurt. And it's come so close to one of my guys punching Dr. Pounder. You should know what's going on."

"What's he doing?"

"Calling us stupid. Telling the guys they don't know what they're doing."

"You leave it to me, I'll deal with it when I go up there today."

Later that afternoon, John cornered Derrick in a railcar used as a makeshift office at the crash site. "And I'll tell you what you're going to do," John said, seething from the perceived insubordination. "You're going to go into Hinton tonight, and get a bottle of rye, and a bottle of scotch, and you're going to invite every one of those guys for a drink."

The look on Derrick's face was enough to tell John he wasn't getting anywhere, and he'd probably be in the market for a new deputy before long. Derrick wasn't his only problem, either. Few remains had emerged from the wreckage and the identification of victims was consequently slow. The families and the media demanded information about the lives lost. There was no manifest, nothing to positively indicate who had actually boarded that train. Tickets may have been purchased by one person and used by another, or purchased on the train after departure. And, other than the two sets of remains found early on, there were no bodies under all the spilled grain, only ash and ice. The Transportation Safety Board and the RCMP had a mystery to solve. Every detail needed notation, and that took time.

After four days, John was becoming annoyed with the constant vigilance of the press at the scene. He asked an RCMP officer why the media was still hanging around relentlessly.

"They want to get a photo of a body being removed," the officer replied.

That pissed John off even more. "Well, let's give it to them, then. I'm tired of dealing with those rubber-neckers. Stuff a body bag with something, pillows or the like, and carry it out on a litter so they can get their snapshot and leave us to work."

Four RCMP officers carried a slumping white body bag out through the rubble while the cameras flashed and snapped. The image took over the story, but not as they had hoped. Within hours, journalists discovered it was a ruse and howled doubly loud for answers.

Two days later, John sat in the dining room of the Westin Hotel reading the Edmonton Journal editorial about his lack of integrity around the fake-body scandal. At the time, it didn't bother him. Just one more bit of drama, but nothing compared to the real work at hand. Disaster scenes, he was learning, were riddled with political potholes. None of his superiors said a word about the bad press. At least he could be thankful for that. He didn't think about the families who might have been clinging to the shape of the body bag in that well-publicized photo.

When the recovery operation was finally complete, there were 23 fatalities and another 95 people injured. Fifty-six days of public hearings failed to identify a specific cause for the head on collision. The accident was attributed to human error, but none of the men at the front of the train had survived to tell their story and solve the mystery definitively. It was an exhaustive and expensive investigation.

* * *

Graeme Dowling started working as a forensic pathologist for the Alberta government in the summer of 1986. He'd seen his first autopsy at the age of twelve when he spent a summer working for the Chief ME in Winnipeg, his hometown. It was the first religious experience of his life, despite a prior Sunday school education. It was obvious to him that the dead body was a shell, not a person. Something fundamental was gone. To Graeme, this was proof of a soul, and therefore, a God.

Dowling completed a ten-week forensic pathology elective with Dr. Butt in Calgary during his third year at medical school. He'd originally signed up to work with Manitoba's Chief ME, Bill Parker, a well-loved leader, but Parker died before Graeme's term started. Dr. Butt had toured the medical school in Winnipeg, and impressed the young student with his forward thinking approach to death investigation. After Dr. Parker's death, Dowling asked to spend his elective time in Alberta with Dr. Butt. Graeme knew early on that forensic pathology was for him. He decided against spending any time in family practice and went straight into his specialty. John helped him secure a position for a formal forensic pathology fellowship in Dallas after his residency in Calgary. Once he finished his education, Graeme was offered a job as Derrick Pounder's assistant—an entry-level forensic pathologist's job. He'd also been offered the Chief ME position for Newfoundland, but he turned it down to return to Calgary. Derrick wanted a thorough foundation before he thought of moving up the ladder administratively. He liked publishing papers and having a focus on the science. The admin side wasn't for him, or so he thought.

"I want you to remember you're reporting to me, not John Butt," Pounder said from the start. Graeme was fine with that. He liked Dr. Pounder, and he got along fine with Dr. Butt, but he knew there was tension between the Chief and his Deputy. Dowling had no intention of running to John with issues. He was ready to get into the science and the mysteries at hand. It wasn't his style to make waves. Graeme was tall but slight, and quiet, even a bit timid compared to the other two pathologists.

Less than a year after Dowling started in earnest with the Edmonton Office of the Chief Medical Examiner, in the summer of 1987, Deputy Chief Derrick Pounder quit. Pounder was obviously unhappy with his boss and he made it clear by telling stories to the media. A news article appeared shortly after Derrick's departure, with negative quotes attributed to the former Deputy Chief. When members of the press scrummed the Minister of Justice, pushing for a retort, the seasoned politician shut them down with two words, "Derrick who?"

Graeme was left holding the reins of the northern Alberta ME operation. It wasn't what he wanted, and he thought of declining the position, but his colleagues encouraged him to take it. Graeme was the kind of guy who listened to cues from the universe, so he eventually took the post as Assistant Deputy Chief Medical Examiner. The title was a mouthful, but Dowling knew Dr. Butt liked specificity. It must have been a vestige of his military training.

Assistant Deputy Chief Dowling was one month into his new position at the helm when a tornado mowed a twisted path through the city of Edmonton. Twenty-six people were killed on a sunny Friday afternoon leading up to a long weekend. The sky had shown ominous indications all day. The tornado touched down in Leduc at 3:25 p.m. For forty kilometres, the funnel, up to one kilometre wide in places, tore up farms, towns, trains, and industries. Cars were plucked from the highway and thrown into fields. Alberta dubbed it "Black Friday," the second most destructive tornado in Canadian history.

Most of the staff were still at the ME's office in Edmonton. Assistant Deputy Dowling was at his desk when the warning came. He gathered everyone into the conference room in one section of the building with no outside walls. The twister ripped through the city, but the Office of the ME wasn't in the path of destruction. Once the danger passed, calls came in for the dead. Dowling sent a team to the first site and headed to the second site, a trailer park.

By the time he arrived, the bodies had been moved to a pizza shop in the nearby strip mall. Whoever had taken charge of the site initially thought it best to designate a temporary morgue and get the bodies out of sight ASAP. Unfortunately, this made investigation and identification more difficult. Graeme assumed the restaurant was chosen because it had heavy drapes and a walk-in refrigeration unit. It wasn't a bad choice, but he felt for the owners of the pizza parlour. The business wouldn't survive the stigma. No one would want to eat pizza there ever again.

Dowling already had one disaster under his belt. In Dallas, he was involved in the recovery effort after a DC 10 crashed and 147 people were killed. He knew what to do, who to notify, and how to go with the flow. He'd called John the first chance he had and was glad for whatever help the Chief offered. Dr. Butt flew up to Edmonton right away and met with Dowling.

"How would you like to approach this? How can I help?" John asked.

The two men split the work with Graeme remaining in charge of the forensic side of things while John handled the higher-ups, the families, and the media through the government's communications department.

When it was all over, the new Assistant Deputy Chief was pleased with the efficiency of the operation. It had gone smoothly. Everyone had been identified within 24 hours. He didn't have any problems with his boss. Far from it, he thought John was great, supportive and helpful. Too bad none of the other pathologists felt that way about Alberta's Chief. Dr. Butt was a perfectionist and a controlling boss, but Dowling found as long as he kept John in the loop with regular updates, he was left to himself.

* * *

It hadn't taken Pat Bruni long to get a sense of Dr. Butt's personality. They quickly developed a bond. She loved his crazy sense of humour. One down day, he marched through the office in an oversized novelty cowboy hat, carrying an upturned metal pot and a large spoon. He high-stepped through the connected rooms, banging and singing at the top of his lungs. Without a word of explanation, and without stopping for a reaction, he marched out the door and headed down the hall to the next office, still singing and banging.

He was so good at acting a part, and he played practical jokes on everyone. She'd almost been shot once because of John's crazy sense of humour. When he wanted to give the rookie cops a good scare, he asked her to slip into a body bag and lay on the autopsy table in the processing room. John told her to take shallow breaths, if any, and to be very still until he coughed. That was her signal to jump up and thrash around.

"Listen, I've had to call you back here because this is a very bad case," John told the officers while Pat, encased in the gauzy bag, tried to hold her breath. "We're dealing with a brutal homicide here, and it's very, very bad." Then he coughed.

Pat did as instructed, moaning and writhing on cue. She was able to see reasonably well through the white fabric as she thrashed her arms. One of the police officers yelled and jumped back. The other went for his gun. John was doubled over laughing.

Pat shouted, "Jeezus! No, don't shoot! Don't shoot! It's me, it's me! Tell them it's me!"

After that dangerous role, it took her awhile to forgive her boss and play along again.

* * *

John thought Graeme had come a long way. He'd been so shy when he was a resident, but he was handling the leadership role well. With cooperative and dutiful Dr. Dowling running the Edmonton operation, John stepped up his mission to spread the scientific gospel of forensic pathology. He wanted to promote the medical examiner system and lecture on the importance of learning from death investigation. Opportunities to speak at international conferences and symposiums were plentiful, and John took full advantage of his position. In his mind, the promotion of his methods in forensic pathology meant the promotion of Alberta and its government's commitment to justice. When the Chief ME position was awarded to John, the wealthy provincial government had been busy educating its people in management skills and administrative best practices. They built two new mortuaries and outfitted their operations with the most current equipment and technology. It was Alberta's golden age.

John had settled into his new home on the hill. He carried on his romance with Mary, though he did break it off briefly to have a fling with a naughty woman who liked to party. But Jessica and Kimberly adored Mary, and the statuesque socialite was a better choice for John's circle of professionals. Mary didn't seem to mind the interlude. She went on dates of her own, but happily reunited with John when the other woman faded out of sight. Once again, John felt a sense of satisfaction. He'd quelled his secret passions, found a suitable second in command for the ME office, and travelled the world for work and pleasure.

On a spring evening, John received a call from a young man named Mark, who claimed to be a friend of Kimberly's.

"Your daughter thinks we'd hit it off," Mark said, by way of introduction. "I travel to Calgary often for work. It'd be nice to have a friend for dinner. I get tired of eating alone all the time!"

John was a little confused, but thought, *What the hell, he sounds interesting enough.* "That sounds fine. I'd be pleased to have a meal with you."

"Great. I look forward to it."

"What did Kimberly tell you about me?" John wondered what had inspired this fellow to reach out.

"She said we have the same sense of humour, so she gave me your number."

Over spicy food at The King & I Thai Cuisine on 11ᵗʰ Avenue in downtown Calgary, John quizzed the young man about his life. Mark Herbert was raised on a small farm in the berry fields of Richmond, BC. He graduated from the British Columbia Institute of Technology with a degree in Marketing Management, and a specialization in Real Estate. He loved living in Vancouver, but the travel bug and his job took him on regular adventures out of town.

Kim had been right about Mark and her Dad. It didn't take them long to get laughing. The two men became fast friends.

Chapter Fourteen

MEMENTO MORI

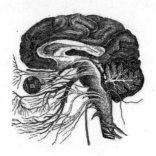

The work of collecting and documenting human remains from the Swissair disaster turns to investigation and discovery. Positive identification is the goal. The ID evidence for each case crosses the Chief ME's boardroom desk before a confirmation is made. If and when the proof meets Dr. Butt's approval, he reaches out to the family and personally confirms their loss. The conversations are difficult. They can quickly go awry. John finds the sorrow infectious. Despite years of experience, he is not inoculated. He has kept away from the grief for most of his career. Maybe there were more important things to do back then, but not now.

A call comes from the Greek Embassy. The family of a female victim has booked a fare for her remains to be flown home to Greece on Saturday. The diplomat on the phone wants to ensure all the arrangements are in place at the morgue. John checks the file. They have identified only a small piece of the victim's jaw. That's it.

"I don't like this idea and I don't think we should release the remains yet," John says to the diplomat. "Do you think the family is prepared to have the casket go up and down every time new remains are found? It's the elevator effect, and that's wrong."

Service Corporation International, the organization hired by Swissair to shepherd, prepare, host, casket, and inter the remains, doesn't agree with the Medical Examiner's opinion. Service Corp, the largest death service provider in the world, a publicly-traded mega company headed by a Texas entrepreneur, isn't going to let some pushy doctor get in the way of their business.

A funeral director from New York, who works for Service Corp., is dispatched to Halifax to deal with arrangements for the remains, and the stubborn Medical Examiner.

"Look, Dr. Butt, you shouldn't be interfering."

"Why is that?" John asks. *You bastards are going to sell them a new casket every time new remains are identified!*

"Families should make these decisions themselves. It's not up to you what happens to the remains after they have been identified."

The family doesn't even know what the fuck is in the casket! John thinks. He doesn't like the direction this is going, but the funeral director has a point. The ME has no say. If the investigation on a piece of flesh or bone is complete, and the family wants to bury that piece, however they may have been misled by the commerce of the death industry, he has no power to hold them back. The piece of jaw goes in the much-too-large casket and is flown to Greece, despite John's protests.

* * *

Bob Conrad hasn't caught or sold any tuna since the disaster. No one wants to buy them anyway. Stories of body parts in the water have made it around the world and back. September is a big month for tuna in these waters, and the crash site is smack dab in the middle of the most lucrative fishing area.

Bob's boat got stuck in Dover after the plane went down. He wasn't able to get back to his own dock the day after the crash. Officials had stopped all marine traffic at the mouth of the bay, and he had to beg a ride in a fish truck. It's a long drive from Dover to his home in French Village, a collection of cozy houses gathered in a huddle beside a craggy bit of coastline. When the fish truck pulled up to the end of his dirt driveway, Bob was exhausted. His neighbour looked out the window as he trudged slowly toward his pale blue home behind the thin stand of deciduous trees. She stepped out on her porch to say hello and Bob went over to her. Not many words were spoken but much was exchanged. She leaned in and gave him a hug. It opened something in Bob, and profound sorrow poured out.

Peggy's Cove, a quaint fishing village, sits 20 minutes down the road from Bob. At the moment, Peggy's Cove is also possessed by the aftermath of the crash. Reporters, family members, looky-loos, and officials of every type, camp around the town. A long line of parked network vans, with their antennae raised high, provides a contemporary contrast to the scenes of seafaring life. The town's narrow roads wind around the rocks, rising and falling past one quaint house after another. The wood is weather-beaten and silver-grey, in harmony with the granite landscape. Wharves lining the rocky seashore are piled with wire lobster cages and dotted with the bright pink, orange, and blue ball-floats that bounce on the water once the cages are set and submerged. Even these bits of fluorescent plastic have muted exteriors, washed to cotton-candy colours by the sea. On the edge of town, a tall, white lighthouse with a red roof and a green light stands watch over the whale's-back arches of stone, warning sailors of danger, and lighting their way home.

Everything is topsy-turvy for Bob and his neighbours around the bay, and everyone around here has the whole sad story in their eyes. Bob's recent connection with David Wilkins over the loss of David's son, Monte, is a light in the lost fisherman's heart. Masculinity loves heroism, but the emotional upheaval in the aftermath has nowhere to go. Women can cry and talk things through, but what does a man do? He doesn't want to be the kind of guy who muscles his way through a tragedy. Bob is able to be honest about his feelings, to be vulnerable, with David. Together, the men are learning how to cry.

* * *

It's crazy how much time John spends on the phone notifying families and dealing with all the organizations involved in the process. Mark's call was a welcome relief, and the best thing that's happened all week. That young man is a true friend. John's daughters were no help. Kimberly has called to talk about her own problems. He told her, "You're not going to bury me six feet under." That was the end of that conversation. And Jessica hasn't called at all. He is bombarded by understanding words and gestures from complete strangers, but his own family offers no support.

Many of the victims' families write letters to the man who stood on stage and cried for them. One, in particular, props John up:

Dear Dr. Butt:

My family was present in Nova Scotia the day after the accident of Swissair flight 111. We had the opportunity to attend a number of briefings regarding the accident and sensed the great load that was on your shoulders.

It was clear that though you had a very difficult and unsavory task to perform, you were more than a forensic pathologist but you were a touched individual with tears in your voice as you reported on what you were finding. Your gentleness and compassion, even when questioned by those who were less than hospitable, sent a testimony to our family of the genuine, compassionate person you are.

I want to thank you for being available to us to ask questions as long as we wanted, and for taking this tragedy so personally. You need to know how much we feel for you in your job, and how important what you are doing is to those of us who are having to cope with the aftermath of this terrible tragedy. We could truly tell that you did feel our pain and share this tragedy with us.

Sincerely,
David and Janet Wilkins

John remembers the Wilkins family. David gave him comfort that Friday night. When the ophthalmologist from California put his arm around John and offered him caring words, he'd solidified the Medical Examiner's resolve to be nothing but honest with the grieving crowd, despite the officious route of his colleagues.

Another letter catches John's attention. It's from a single woman who lost her only child in the crash. She's flown home to New York, but wants to come back and help with clerical work in the ME's office, or with the Transportation Safety Board (TSB) investigation. She has a graduate degree and a good skill set. Obviously, this woman wants to feel useful, and she's eager to be involved. He'll ask Linda about it.

* * *

"I've been talking to a woman, and her daughter was on the plane. She wants to be in here—" Dr. Butt says.

"Not going to happen," Linda says, interrupting.

"Well, she wants to be part of it. To feel better."

"We're not into feeling better. We're into doing a job, and the two can't mix." Linda can't believe her ears. Some people think Dr. Butt is full of himself. Some men—men who've spent day after day in the thick of the horror—don't think Dr. Butt should have so much notoriety. Linda agrees with them. What's he done that's so much more important than anyone else? Why is he crying about it in front of the world? Here he is trying to bring family members into the morgue, for goodness sake.

"I thought she could help out in the comfort lounge somehow, not right in the morgue." Dr. Butt presses her to agree.

"What, so after someone does this traumatic work with these bits of bodies, then they go into the lounge and sit with a mother whose daughter is somewhere out in the bay?"

"Well, I guess not ..."

"What happens when we go for a break and someone says something horrible but funny and we all laugh? No one will even go in that lounge if you put a family member in there."

"I suppose that's true. But can't we find something for—"

"No. You can't even bring that woman on the property. It's just not fair." Mixing mourners with the morgue isn't going to happen on her watch.

For a smart man, her boss can sure be a dummy. It's not their job to be mollycoddling the grieving. And now Dr. Butt is calling all the families to let them know when they have positive identification of a victim. That's the RCMP's job! The plane was chock full of rich people, important people. *Of course, Dr. Butt wants to rub shoulders with those international muckety-mucks*, she thinks. *That's why he insists on making the calls.*

* * *

The media storm whips up one horrible detail after another, then churns the headlines out to the world. Journalists and reporters come from around the globe. Residents around St. Margaret's Bay are incessantly pestered. The fishermen who left their warm beds to head out on the dark water when the plane went down are paying for their bravery with a loss of privacy. Locals give their hearts to the grief while shielding their faces and the stricken families from the cameras. The world is waiting, wanting, eager for information, groping for answers.

Terrorism is still on the table. The RCMP approach everything with necessary suspicion. Theories of possible crimes pour out of the evidence. Flight 111 has often been referred to as the United Nations run. The plane takes off from New York, bound for Geneva. Many of the passengers are professionals, leaders, and academics. The cargo hold is loaded with jewels, cash, and priceless art. Some of the wounds on the victims are consistent with buckshot damage. The shattered condition of the remains also points to the possibility of a bomb.

Ten days into the disaster investigation, Major Crimes Constable Rick Chadwick awakes at home after his first decent night's sleep since he was called to duty on *HMCS Preserver*. After seven days at sea sorting, documenting, and chaperoning body parts to the morgue, the recovery of the remains slowed. Chadwick was pulled from the ship and sent to canvass residents around the bay. It was obviously a holding-pattern placement. Within the hour, he was yanked from door-to-door and tossed on a flight to New York, armed with a video camera and a mission: film every inch, inside and out, of the MD-11 flying to NYC from Switzerland.

During his plane ride home the next morning, the Mountie was uncomfortable sitting so close to all the civilians and their raw emotions. It felt like he was on the wrong side of the curtain. But now he's home, in bed with his beautiful wife, recharged and ready for the next assignment. *Finally I'll get to blend in with the rest of the investigation*, he thinks. *The crazy part is over.*

Rick pulls into a parking space behind Hangar A where the RCMP Investigator's area is set up. He's hoping his new assignment is a good one—something with a little less stress and running around. One of his buddies coordinates all the plane parts that come in to Hangar A. That guy gets to go home at night and sleep in his own bed. It sounds about right to Rick after his ordeal at sea.

"Oh good, you're here." Rick's boss approaches him in the parking lot before he can get into the hangar and say hi to the investigation team and catch up on what his compatriots have been doing.

Rick doesn't like the tone in his boss's voice. "What now?" he asks, expecting the worst.

The sergeant drapes his burly arm around the young man's shoulder. "Come walk with me," he says, guiding Chadwick toward Hangar B where the morgue is in full swing. "Have I got a job for you."

Oh, great, Rick thinks, *so much for blending in.*

"We've run into a little trouble over at the morgue and we need someone there to represent us, look at how our operation is set up, and see if we can do it differently."

Rick reads between the lines. He knows his boss wants the RCMP to be in control of the investigation. If there is a crime here, and it ends up in court, every little detail counts. Things must be getting out of hand over there. Constable Chadwick, contrary to his hopes, is heading back to body parts and the big drama.

The morgue in Hangar B is a mini city filled with marshmallow people in white paper suits. Military and local doctors, nurses, and x-ray technicians mingle with Navy, RCMP, and TSB staff. There must be at least 20 police officers already here as the "next-of-kin" group, answering calls in the 1-800-number phone bank across the hall from the grisly functioning part of the morgue. Rick sees right away that Dr. Butt is the king of this underworld. Butt sits at the head of the boardroom table and hands out rules, assignments, and identities. When the sergeant introduces Chadwick to Dr. Butt as the new RCMP liaison, the confident young Constable has already assessed the situation and knows to play to the Medical Examiner's ego.

"I'll do my best to stay out of your way, but what I'd like to do is learn from what you're doing here. I'm looking over our operation to make sure it's efficient so we can get the best work out of our members." Rick smiles. His dark hair is combed straight back and smooth. His shirt is clean and pressed. He smells fresh.

Butt obliges the introduction, but doesn't engage. He appears distracted. Proof of positive IDs await approval from the Chief Medical Examiner and Rick is sure John won't let any claim go by uninspected, for now. He has to get this situation under control. The RCMP should be in charge of this whole operation.

Rick sits in on an identification notification and can't believe what he's seeing. Butt is crying right in front of him! The old doc is engaged in some big conversation with a family member, and he's blubbering away. *There's no way he can handle this through the entire plane load of people*, Rick thinks. There's a whole team of RCMP officers with special training in the room right next door, ready and waiting. *How am I going to get him away from this?* After watching a few of these calls unfold in the same manner, Rick takes action.

"This must be a difficult process for you," he says. "I'm wondering if there is some other way we could do it, because your time is so valuable. You need to be on the floor, coordinating with your folks, making the big decisions." Chadwick suggests they single out a few of the ladies in the phone bank to be on a special notification team. The people answering calls at the information centre are RCMP members and Medical Examiner Investigators, and they are all women. At the end of Rick's explanation, he can tell old Butt is warming to the idea. If step one is re-establishing authority with the families, he can check that off his list. This may all be easier than expected.

* * *

Things with the RCMP upstart Chadwick go fairly well for the first week or so. John doesn't mind having him about. It was handy to have him work out the family notifications. The women over in the phone bank, the ones Rick trained, they're doing a fine job now. People still call and ask for "Dr. Butt" personally. He can't walk away from that connection. He still talks with family members when they call for him, but those conversations are usually easier than the notification-of-identification calls.

The wife of the pilot from Swissair 111 asks to see the ME when she flies in from Switzerland. John meets with her at the little brown chapel on the naval base. The wife brings another woman whose boyfriend was also part of the crew.

"My boyfriend wore a ring. I'm hoping I can have it back if it has been found?" the young woman asks. Her question is directed at John.

"Well, I don't see why not. Let me make a call and see if we have it," John replies without hesitation. These women have flown all the way from Switzerland hoping for a little solace or some kind of understanding. He can't give them the bodies. If this young lady wants to go home with a memento of her heart's desire, then the good doctor is willing to oblige.

John has had it with the RCMP anyway. They still insist on treating this as a bloody criminal investigation. The divers found the voice recorder already and know there was a fire in the cockpit. The TSB guys in Hangar A working on the wreckage are talking about arcing between the wires and flammable insulation. Even though there's nothing going out officially, these cops could stand to lighten up a bit and have some compassion.

John knows Rick is not going to be happy about this ring thing.

The law says the ME *may* place evidence in the hands of the police, but it doesn't say he *must*. The two investigative bodies try to define the statutes through constant interpretive struggles.

John asks Chadwick to check the inventory and see if the ring has been found.

"Dr. Butt, we can't deal with that right now."

"No. I want to know."

"We don't have the ring."

"You can't say that. You haven't even checked."

Rick remembers his job is to lubricate the situation with the ME. "Fine. I'll ask." He can read that old bully's mind. Butt wants to give that ring back.

First, Rick calls to see if the ring has been found. Maybe it's not even there, and problem solved. Two minutes later, he hears back—affirmative, the ring is in inventory. *Isn't that special*, Rick thinks. *Now what?*

He doesn't tell Dr. Butt right away. He decides to run this problem up the chain of command and see where it stops.

"I know what's going to happen," Rick says to his higher-up. "I'm going to tell him we have this ring and he's going to try and take it. That can't happen."

"No. That's not going to happen." The RCMP officer in charge of the Swissair investigation agrees with Rick, but he wants to check with his higher-ups, too.

Back at the morgue, Dr. Butt confronts the RCMP liaison. "Well? Do we have it?"

"There's a ring, but you can't have it. It's part of a crime scene investigation." Chadwick stands his ground.

"I'll get that ring. It's under my jurisdiction, and I'll get it."

"No, you won't. It's evidence and we're keeping it."

"I want that ring and I'm calling the CrOps officer to get it!"

Not long after Butt storms off to tattle, Rick finds himself on the phone with the Nova Scotia RCMP Criminal Operations Officer, or CrOps. Essentially, this guy's the top dog. "Give that ring to the Medical Examiner," is the order from above.

The next day, Constable Chadwick arrives at the Lord Nelson hotel bearing the ring. He isn't happy about it. RCMP rules require absolute loyalty to command, so here he is, smiling while handing over a piece of potential evidence to a foreign civilian.

CHAPTER FIFTEEN

BODY OF SECRETS

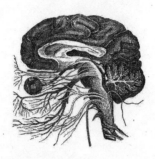

JOHN'S RELATIONSHIP WITH Mark Herbert grew to a kindred friendship, much to the dismay of a few key women in John's life. In John's opinion, this outgoing young man had a constantly positive attitude and a symbiotic sense of humour with the older doctor. Mark wasn't flustered by irreverence or shocked by pointedness. He was handsome and athletic, with broad shoulders, and a wide grin over a square jaw.

John had taken up swimming to stay fit after developing hip issues in his mid-fifties and he invited his new friend to join him at the pool when Mark was in town for business.

"You just want to see him naked in the changing rooms," Mary said.

She has a point, John thought, but admitted nothing to Mary.

John and Mark's incidental meetings became planned getaways before long. The pair travelled well together. They shared a love of fine food and drink, and most essential, a thirst for adventure. They went out to bars as two single guys and John played wingman for his mate. Mark was the true friend John had unknowingly yearned for since Alex told him off and left him standing on the sidewalk near the junior high school in a confused daze. The rebuff had stung more than any of his mother's slaps. Forty years later, Mark had unlocked the door to John's private store of himself. He knew, eventually, he'd have to tell Mark the truth.

Mary didn't seem to like John spending time with his new best buddy. She was still an enjoyable companion, but John didn't like any sense of ownership implied with the term partner. He wanted the relationship to stay light, despite a decade spent dancing the night away at various galas and camping in the country together on family vacations. John found ways to let Mary know where she stood. They went for drives in the countryside of Alberta's patchwork foothills. Mary liked to sit in the front and gaze over the landscape. On one Sunday drive, with Jessica along, John offered the front seat to his daughter and handily supplanted one woman wrestling for attention with another.

At 57 years of age, Dr. Butt was at the top of his career game. He'd been elected President of the National Association of Medical Examiners in the USA, or NAME, despite his Canadian citizenship and practice. John was known in the States for his freelance consulting work, and several years earlier, he'd started consulting in areas outside of his Alberta jurisdiction to supplement his income now that he was supporting two households. He was often hired by defence lawyers from other provinces or countries to re-evaluate autopsy evidence during the appeal process. The possibility of righting a wrong and freeing someone who was unjustly imprisoned proved entirely enticing.

His work with NAME, his consulting work, and various speaking engagements kept him in the jet-set life. In 1990, he took two full months off work and travelled the globe. First he went to England for a visit with his aunt, then flew to the Middle East for a military fix while Operation Desert Storm raged, and travelled to a toxicology conference and a forensic pathology meeting in Australia. From there, John flew to speaking engagements in Thailand, Malaysia, and Singapore. Dr. Butt's mission to increase the presence of forensic pathology in the academic community worldwide was on track. He took short, two-week sabbaticals yearly, along with his holiday weeks, and used them to spread the good word of doctors as highly qualified death investigators. Everybody, it seemed, wanted to hear what he had to say, and he was only too happy to oblige.

* * *

For five years, Assistant Deputy Chief Medical Examiner Graeme Dowling struggled to fill his autopsy suite with qualified forensic pathologists—they'd heard of Dr. Butt's reputation for unreasonable expectations and public humiliations. But Graeme found his boss reasonably easy to work with. The role of Assistant Deputy Chief had been foisted on Dowling shortly after he started his career. He made a habit of weekly check-ins with John because he liked the support. Graeme was young, and didn't want to do anything stupid. Though he felt entirely confident in his medical, investigative, and scientific skills, government protocol and policy were still fuzzy issues. John often told Graeme that the phone check-ins were appreciated, and the Edmonton ME was left unmolested as a result.

But Dowling couldn't run the northern office on his own. The leadership role required hours of administration, and the dead kept coming. He needed qualified doctors to perform autopsies. With John now sitting at the head of an international forensic pathology organization, everyone in the field knew his name, and his reputation for utter control and perfection. After several futile interviews with prospective forensic pathologists, Graeme went over his boss's head to the Deputy Minister of Justice, Neil McCrank.

"Sir, I want you to know I have absolutely no problems working with Dr. Butt, but I think you need to know about this. I can't hire people because of him."

McCrank listened, but appeared unmoved. Perhaps he didn't know of John's reputation. As far as Graeme was aware, the officials in charge thought John was the perfect man for the job.

Graeme pushed on. He wanted to make his position clear. "The pathologists don't say anything about why they're really leaving for fear they won't get hired elsewhere. They make up a story about another opportunity. But I can tell you that's not why they left."

"There are always personality conflicts in high-stress environments," McCrank said.

"Do me one favour," Graeme said. "Next time one of our forensic paths quits, could you please look into it personally?"

"I can do that," McCrank replied. Then, after a moment, added: "But I want you to know that I'm behind John one hundred percent. He's the Chief."

* * *

In the summer of 1992, the year before John's contract with the Government of Alberta was set to renew for the fifth time, fifteen years after the Alberta medical examiner system was realized, and seventeen years after he'd started with the Alberta government, Neil McCrank's secretary called John to set a meeting.

Another pathologist had quit. The personnel department called the departing doctor for an exit interview and Neil followed through on his promise to Graeme. It came down to Dr. Butt's overbearing attitude. The outgoing pathologist confirmed everything that Graeme had said. Working for Dr. Butt was stressful and often humiliating. Doctors who had spent years studying and specializing weren't willing to make the sacrifice, especially since opportunities for forensic pathologists in North America were plentiful.

Neil appeared in a bad mood from the moment John arrived at the Deputy Minister's office. "You've lost too many pathologists." The Deputy Minister didn't waste any time getting to it.

John flushed. He'd been working with Neil for three years already, and they'd been fine. He liked the man, even felt friendly toward him. There was always the matter of how far to let someone in. Appearances are easier to keep up from a distance. John fidgeted, compulsively raising his hand to his ear and stroking the curve of its helix.

"We won't be hiring a replacement for Dr. Roy," McCrank said. "The recruitment is too expensive. We can't keep hiring."

John was devastated. This meant he was to be the only forensic pathologist in the Calgary office. He felt as if everything he had created was crumbling. Did he work for seventeen years building this system to be tied to an autopsy table? Neil was nice, but he was also newer and younger than John. He hadn't been around through the years of sweat equity. A wave of panic replaced the initial shock and hurt feelings. He left McCrank's office in a daze, unable to contribute any defence, or possible solution.

John took time to think. He gathered statistics on death investigation needs per capita, hoping to convince Neil that one forensic pathologist for the southern half of Alberta was ludicrous. Then he started on his back-up plan, sending resumes out to various choice locations in southern BC, his preferred locale, should things fall apart.

At their next meeting, Neil didn't take kindly to John's presentation of data. He appeared angry, and John's initial flustered reaction was soon replaced by indignation. John prepared to lock horns, but the Deputy Minister swept that issue aside. After discarding the ME's research, McCrank outlined another big problem, as he saw it.

"The justice department needs a stay-at-home Chief Medical Examiner." The Minister continued on this line, citing specific examples of John's extra time off to promote forensic pathology and the medical examiner system to the international community. "You are the Chief Medical Examiner of Alberta, not the world."

Neil was obviously determined to clip John's wings and keep him in the morgue. McCrank referred to his own pile of stats. He outlined all of the trips John had taken and his extra days off here and there over the past three years. The perceived pettiness made John furious.

"If we can't come to some agreement on these issues, we won't be renewing your contract." McCrank's final blow was fatal, and it killed John's desire to continue as Alberta's Chief Medical Examiner. After seventeen years at the top, his reign in Alberta was about to end.

* * *

Nurse Investigator Pat Bruni adored her boss, but there was something about him she couldn't quite put her finger on. She saw him rip others apart if they did anything wrong, and he had trouble with almost everyone in the office at one time or another. *He must be fighting with some inner demons*, she thought. For some reason, Dr. Butt never scolded her.

Pat had gay friends, and she talked about them openly. She thought John might be gay, too, but there was no way she was going to ask him. It's not like she'd heard any rumours about him. It was subtler than that. There was that time he'd called and pretended to be the lover of a gay man whose body came through the morgue after he'd hung himself.

"I'm so heartbroken," Dr. Butt said, sobbing between affected words impregnated with a feminine lilt. "How will I live without him?"

Pat did her best to soothe the poor fellow on the other end of the line. She had a wealth of experience behind her now. Dealing with people's grief was a privilege. She'd learned that meeting someone in their darkest place gave an intimate view of the heart without the social façade of the mind.

The distraught lover's voice cracked a bit, like he was suppressing a laugh. Pat pulled the phone away from her ear and looked down at the call display. It was the morgue's number. When she put the receiver back to her ear, her boss was laughing so hard he couldn't talk.

"You bastard!" She screamed at him and slammed down the receiver. She was mad, but only because he really had her fooled. It took her some time to forgive him, yet again. But they'd become friends over the years working together, and they shared a macabre but witty sense of humour. She loved to laugh, and John's jokes were hard to resist.

Lately, though, he was no fun at all. He'd stopped his pranks and impromptu performances. He hardly laughed. To make matters worse, one of the pathologists from Edmonton had mysteriously shown up at the Calgary office and thrown the order of things off balance. Pat noticed that Dr. Butt didn't even look at the other doctor, and she didn't see them speak to one another. Usually, Dr. Butt micro-managed the forensic paths, so what was the deal with this new guy? *Geeze, forensic pathologists have the biggest egos*, she thought. Something was going on and it didn't feel good at all.

* * *

The year John spent finishing his contract in the Calgary office was painful. He'd handed his resignation to Neil after the ultimatum, but didn't tell any of his staff. Everyone was still tense, sensing their leader's discomfort. Not long before John left, Neil sent an Edmonton pathologist down to take over the management of the Calgary office. When John's contract ended, Graeme Dowling was named the new Chief ME of Alberta, and Edmonton took over Alberta's Office of the Chief Medical Examiner designation. John's era was over.

The stress and shame weighed heavily on John, so he started seeing Dr. Gary Sanders, a psychiatrist in the family therapy unit at the hospital. Gary and John had met informally years earlier and John knew Dr. Sanders was openly gay.

The psychiatrist's office was small, with a melamine and metal desk pushed against one wall and two tubular chairs. The floors were covered in a bland carpet and one long, narrow window in the corner presented a view of the parking lot. John and Gary sat face to face while the doctor asked probing questions and the patient bit the tip of his finger and wiggled in his chair.

"I see in your file you've spent time in hospital for psychiatric care."

"Yes. Years ago. I had an unusual episode one morning and called the police because I panicked. There was never any explanation for my episode. The doctors called it stress and said I'd be fine. I try to be more aware now. That's why I'm here."

John told Sanders about the tension with his wife when he was a younger man, how she refused to talk to him even when John's father was visiting, how embarrassed he was by it, how he smashed the plate, and woke to the experience of being two. "What does that sound like to you?" he asked the psychiatrist.

"That sounds like loneliness. Profound loneliness," Sanders replied.

The same year John lost his job, in 1992, another Calgary man also found himself unemployed. Delwin Vriend, a teacher at a Christian college, was fired after the College President conducted an inquisition and exposed the teacher's sexual inclination. The College Board took no pains to hide their disgust at his homosexual orientation once it came to light, and boldly cited it as the reason for Vriend's dismissal. When Vriend appealed to the Alberta Human Rights Commission for support on the basis of discrimination, they told him sexual orientation was not protected under the *Alberta Individual Rights Protection Act.*

Even though the federal government was lifting the ban on homosexuals in the military, and Justice Minister Kim Campbell introduced a bill to add sexual orientation to the *Human Rights Act,* the province of Alberta was staunchly holding its ground on Christian family values. John certainly wasn't fired for being gay, but suppressing his sexuality was the key stressor that created disparate inner and outer personas—a recipe for extreme psychological dysfunction. It's unlikely he'd have risen to his place of importance in Alberta if he'd been true to himself, but the pressure of maintaining the pretense and suppressing his nature had lost John his job anyway. He had been indoctrinated with the idea that homosexual men were lesser men, starting with his mother insisting he never be a sissy, never show too much emotion, never be soft.

Dr. Sanders slowly coaxed his new patient through conversations about sexuality, but he waited for John to come to his own conclusions. It didn't take Gary long to locate his patient's hidden heart. Classic, open-ended questions about friends, family, and childhood led the conversation to Alex.

"Tell me about him."

"He was very, very good looking: big, but not stocky, and tall with black hair and a round face. We were twelve when we started to pal around, but he was a year behind me in school. He was my neighbour."

"What sorts of things did you do together?"

"We rode bikes, walked the train tracks, went on adventures. The usual."

"He seems to hold an important spot in your memory. Why do you think he's still on your mind?"

"We were best buddies."

"Did you have any physical encounters with him?"

"Yes."

"Of a sexual nature?"

"Yes."

"Well, maybe he was gay."

"I don't think so. I asked him once when we were fooling around if he was thinking about boys or girls. He said girls."

"How did the friendship end?"

"I saw him on Elbow Drive one day, close to where we lived. I'd started high school that year and he was still in a junior school, so we didn't see each other as much. He was walking with another boy I knew. I said something to him that I thought was sort of fetching; that I thought might make him interested. But it didn't."

"Were you hurt?"

"I was disappointed."

Dr. Sanders continued to draw out details of John's feelings. Then, he delivered the revelatory diagnosis. "John, I think you were in love with Alex."

The doctor's words—suggesting Alex was gay, or John was in love with Alex—felt permissive of the ideas themselves. It shifted something in John's thinking.

"Why don't you write a letter to Alex? I don't want you to mail it. I just want you to write it."

For the first time in his life, at the age of 58, John had permission to love a man. When he wrote the letter to Alex, he officially gave himself permission to be a man who loved men. Then he tucked the letter in a drawer and told no one else. He needed more time.

But there was a catalyst. John had fallen in love with Mark, and those buried feelings insisted on themselves once again. John desperately wanted to be honest, but he was afraid of the outcome. Mark was obviously interested in women, and was much younger, and would never take John as a lover. For the first time in his life, he felt he had to tell a straight male friend that he was gay in order to save the friendship.

John was also facing an uncertain financial future. He needed to make some money. Pathfinder Forum, John's consulting company, rented its first bricks-and-mortar office in downtown Calgary, and focused on building the business. That winter, Jessica flew back from the coast to spend time with her dad for Christmas. The father-daughter duo spent an evening making wreaths in John's Park Hill dining room.

"I'm really worried about you, Dad. How are you doing here all alone?" Jessica asked.

John's younger daughter, Kimberly, had also moved to the coast and John lived by himself in an empty dream house. "I'm feeling terrible. I can't keep going like this."

"What? Why, what's wrong?"

"I love Mark," John said. Tears filled his lower lids.

"What are you talking about?"

"Mark has been such a good friend to me through this whole thing. He's been there for me."

Jessica didn't react, and John wasn't ready to be clear, so the conversation ended there. She obviously didn't want to hear about her dad's feelings for her little sister's ex-boyfriend. Jessica and John were cut from the same upper-middle class cloth: reputations were important and scandal was to be avoided. Don't ask, don't tell.

CHAPTER SIXTEEN

ACCOLADES & CONDEMNATIONS

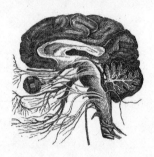

TEN DAYS INTO the Swissair investigation, on the second Friday, the Chief Medical Examiner returns home for the first time since the night of the crash. It's a long journey from Shearwater in Dartmouth back to his house on the hill above the sea, back to the view of St. Margaret's Bay from the living room picture window, to his dogs Ben and Deputy, and his friends across the way. The drive is worth it. Time at home keeps him centered and helps him sleep. He's made it this far without the buzzing, or the horror that follows. The crying is awkward, but so far manageable.

At the end of September, four weeks post-crash, John takes his suitcase home and commutes daily to Shearwater. The morgue and the Medical Examiner's operation in Hangar B are running fairly smoothly: systems in place and protocols followed, identifications and a clear line of communication to families, records in order, and everyone knows their job. The flow of human remains, once constant, has slowed to a trickle. Several hundred pounds of identified bone and flesh, and the thousands of pounds still waiting for processing, are housed in thirteen refrigerated trailers sitting outside an airplane hangar by the sea. On October 1st, the reefer rental company calls to say they need four of their trailers back. It's time to deliver Thanksgiving turkeys. It costs the ME's Office $1700 per trailer to properly sanitize each one before they can be returned. More refrigerated railcars take their place.

Deputy Minister Gordon Gillis asks the ME to attend a meeting with the RCMP. John assumes it's an organizational or up-date meeting, but he's wrong. Six senior officers run through John like a course of salts. He's blindsided by their criticism of his work style. They say he's too controlling, too bossy, and too emotional.

At the end of the dressing-down, the Chief Superintendent lists off his demands. "First," he says, addressing John, "you're going to cooperate with us and share the information we need. Second, we're going to contract that morgue, and give the hangar back to the base. And if you don't like it, you're on your own. No more support from us."

The RCMP at the morgue maintain the database of remains, with records from discovery through the many steps to identification. Without that support, John's well-lubricated machine grinds to a confused halt. It's absolutely unacceptable.

"Well, that's fine," John says. "Then I'm taking all of the identified remains out to the Public Works yard in the country, and I'll move back to my office in town. Then the base can be rid of us altogether. That's no problem, no problem at all."

While it's John's job to return the identified remains to the family members in this scenario, the police investigation has an interest in the recovered remains yet to be processed. And the ME knows his governing law to the letter. The RCMP have zero ability to pull out of the situation. *The Fatalities Enquires Act* won't allow it.

* * *

After the meeting, Gordon Gillis gets to work on damage control. Overseeing the RCMP and the Medical Examiner's Office is like trying to parent unruly teens. They need to quell the flames or they'll have a PR nightmare on their hands. Heaven forbid the press hears that the ME and the RCMP are playing tug of war with victim remains.

Gordon calls John and invites him, plus Ben and Deputy, to his country home for the weekend. The Deputy Minister and the Chief Medical Examiner tromp through the woods to the trout-stocked pond for some fishing. John takes his out his mini scalpel and performs a fish autopsy. He points out the lividity patterns left by the blades of grass pressing on the dead flesh as the blood pools, then spreads out the internal organs and interprets what they have to say about the fish. Gordon thoroughly enjoys it. Whatever the complainers may say about John, they can't dispute his skill as a man of science.

The weekend gives Gordon a chance to ease into conversations about the tension with the RCMP. All evidence in a civil matter has to be objective, and the RCMP are integral to the process, as is the Medical Examiner. It's going to be exhausting if they don't work together. It's a tricky situation for police because they have to be in charge, but they also have to work with the Medical Examiner. The ME is entitled to tell them what he needs, and to give them instructions. And the TSB is entitled to do the same. If push comes to shove and the TSB or the Office of the ME demand more, because it's written in the law, the RCMP have to cooperate.

"You know this is based on legislation," John says to his boss. "For example, what we are doing here is identification. All we're doing is identifying people on the basis of a piece of provincial legislation. The *Vital Statistics Act* requires a death certificate with a bona fide name on it. That's what we're doing here. We're not solving a crime and everybody knows it."

"Well you may be wrong about the applicable legislation. Remember, this crash occurred offshore." Gordon implies the accident may have happened in international waters.

"If that's the case, why are they using Nova Scotia death certificates?" John asks.

It's a rhetorical question. If the crash occurred in non-provincial waters, beyond the border of Nova Scotia's seafaring jurisdiction, Canada's national political machine should be managing, and funding, the disaster recovery efforts. But the Government of Canada doesn't issue death certificates; that's a provincial responsibility. It's up to the Nova Scotia government to cover the bill.

"I wish you wouldn't make issues about it." Gordon keeps his voice calm. "I would prefer that you don't go and talk about this anymore. I think you've got the Swiss flu."

Crankiness is endemic in these situations. He's trying to gently let John know it's time to let go. So many professionals are burned out from working in the aftermath of the Swissair disaster that the term Swiss flu is in common use, and everybody within the ranks knows what it means. You've had too much.

John guffaws at the joke but doesn't say anything in response. Gordon isn't sure if he's having any success in his mission.

Around the time that John and the RCMP are fighting over guardianship of the remains, Deputy Minister Gillis and a few other judicial-political types are trying to figure out what to do with the trailers of unidentified human parts. It's obvious by the sheer quantity remaining that everyone on board will be positively identified long before each of those pieces is processed. Some of the family members think every bit of flesh and bone, every hair, should be identified and repatriated. But the Nova Scotia government is already millions of dollars into the recovery operation. There is no fiscally feasible way to accomplish that task. It would take another year or two, and many expensive DNA tests. The lab in Ottawa would cease to be of use to the rest of the investigators in Canada. It would be swimming with samples from thousands of fragments in various states of decay.

The Honorable Lorne Clarke, the recently retired Chief Justice for Nova Scotia, is appointed to the position of Chair of the Memorial Advisory Committee of Swissair Flight 111, formed to address the issue of handling those inevitable unidentified remains. They start by asking questions. They ask the community, the families, the religious leaders, the airline, and anyone else who may have thoughts on, or be touched by, the outcome. It will take months to formulate a plan that engenders consensus.

* * *

Not long after the tense meeting with the RCMP, the head of the TSB makes an appointment to see John. When he insists John go along with the RCMP and do as they direct, it doesn't go over well. John is starting to feel terribly singled out by all of these alpha males. Maybe he is overstepping with his emotional engagement, but the RCMP are the ones trying to take control from everyone. Whatever Gillis may have done to salvage the situation has just been undone. John is even more determined to stand his ground. No one is taking over his operation while he's in charge.

On the afternoon of Friday, October 9th, John orders his team to stand down. For 37 consecutive days, Hangar B has been alive with men and women working to solve the puzzles of identity in death. Thanksgiving long weekend offers the perfect opportunity to take a break. But on Friday afternoon, when everyone is packing up to head home for a much-needed rest, John notices Chadwick still hard at work.

"Where are you going for the long weekend?" John asks, trying to sound friendly and nonchalant.

"I'm staying here."

"But we're standing down for the holiday. What about your family?" It's making his blood boil to see Chadwick and his moustache defying the order.

"Too much to do," Rick replies.

John stomps off thinking young Chadwick is trying to build stripes. If the man in charge says stand down, then you stand down. Rick alone in the morgue for three days makes the ME nervous.

"Chadwick isn't going home for the weekend. What's that all about?" John asks Linda. "What about his wife and kids?"

"Well, how do I know?" she replies.

"He's one cop I would never, ever want to run into. He's cold, calculating, and humourless."

Linda chuckles, then adds a drop of fuel. "He told me his mother still irons his shirts."

* * *

Constable Chadwick is happy to have the morgue operation largely to himself for a few days. When he was assigned the role of RCMP Liaison with the Medical Examiner's Office for the duration of the investigation, he was tasked with two jobs: get control of communications, and get the autopsy evidence. Rick remembers his Commander's directive, "I know you can do it. Weasel your way in there."

Chadwick has wrestled most of the family communication away from Dr. Butt. Time to move on to the second part of the operation. The RCMP has all the information from conversations with the families, and everything from the Transportation Safety Board, but not the Medical Examiner's files.

The second task might prove a little trickier, however, and these few days alone will allow him to formulate some kind of plan. He has to sneak into the ME's file system and copy the documents. The RCMP believe they need every bit of information, and Dr. Butt isn't letting them have the autopsy files. When Rick asks Linda if he can take the files to the RCMP office to make copies, she resolutely refuses. "Those files are the property of our Office and they're staying secure, right where they are."

Autopsy files are the property of the Office of the Medical Examiner. Though the RCMP can view the files, they must not remove or copy anything. This isn't good enough for the crime fighters. They want everything in their possession permanently.

But Chadwick isn't giving up that easily. He's been tasked with a job and he's not going to let his superiors down, so he befriends David, the ME's file technician.

"David, you don't come in on the weekends, do you?" Rick asks.

"No."

"And the files could be left unlocked if we need to use them on Saturday and Sunday?"

"Yes."

"So ... if I was to scan them on weekends and you didn't come in and didn't know about it, would that matter?"

"I don't care what you do," David says.

Rick takes the response as an open invitation. On subsequent weekends, he sends a tech guy from the RCMP to go in and scan all the ME's Swissair autopsy files. So far, so good.

* * *

At the end of October, David Wilkins receives the official call from Nova Scotia's Office of the Chief Medical Examiner. Dr. Wilkins sits in his ophthalmology office during a break between surgeries and listens to the deep and quiet tones of Dr. Butt confirming the recovery and identification of his son's remains. Of course, Dr. Wilkins already knows his youngest child, nineteen-year-old Monte, has died in the plane crash. But knowledge and belief can be disparate.

"We can send you the official pathology report detailing exactly what we have recovered and how the remains were identified. Some people don't want to know, but some do." The Medical Examiner's voice is steady and soothing.

David remembers Dr. Butt at the podium, struggling with their loss, and how it soothed them all. He yearns for any connection to his lost son. They've recovered a brown deck shoe containing Monte's foot. David had lent the topsiders to his son for the trip.

"Please send me everything. The shoe as well." David hangs up the phone and stays in his office with the door firmly closed. He needs a moment alone before the next surgery. He needs to call his wife.

* * *

By mid November, the makeshift infrastructure of Hangar B's morgue is dismantled and trashed. The smell permeates every board, box, and piece of plastic. Very little is salvageable. The excellent, efficient Public Works crew build a new wood-structure morgue off the side of Hangar A, where the ongoing reassembly of twisted metal on an airplane-shaped wire cage will continue for months and months. John refers to the new, contracted morgue as the "shack" or "the tin pot." The shack is single-story with a gently peaked roof, and a long profile. The main building is about twenty by forty feet. The refrigeration trailers of unidentified remains, sitting side-by-side, attach to a lean-to style enclosed porch that runs the length of the wood structure. It is an endoskeleton of two-by-four wooden ribs with tarpaper and white plastic skin crouched against the massive metal hangar from which it springs.

John has the trailers of identified remains moved to a 220-volt equipped warehouse in the woods, fifteen kilometres outside of Halifax. The RCMP want to keep all of the remains at Shearwater, but they have nowhere inside to store them, so the ME gets his way. John and Linda, for the most part, are back to work at the Halifax Office. At this point, there is little call for the Chief ME at the makeshift morgue. No new human remains come in. But DNA tests can take weeks, so not everyone has been identified yet. Many more samples have to be sent to Ottawa for processing.

John feels sluggish back in his rinky-dink office after the hub-bub of Shearwater. He's never worked anywhere like that marvel of a make-do morgue, and he doubts he ever will again. So many excellent people were working together for a common end, each bringing unique expertise to the task. His oblong room in the QEII building on the edge of the Dalhousie campus feels even smaller than before. The budget, always the budget, is ever and even more of an issue. *How can I keep this up?* he thinks, and the smallness presses against him, and makes him feel dark inside.

By December 11th, a little over three months from the crash date, all the passengers and crew are accounted for through some form of verified identification of some large or small part of who they once were. Roughly 15,000 pieces have been analyzed to reach 228 positive identifications, with an identical twin counting as the 229th victim. Coincidentally, a party to thank everyone involved in the recovery operation has also been planned for Dec. 11th. There are drink tickets, nibbles, and a podium for thank-you speeches or large-scale, long-winded goodbyes.

At the beginning of the event, John is called to speak to the crowd of hundreds. Most of them cheer. His speech is short and full of gratitude for everyone's excellent efforts in this trying time. The room erupts in cheers accompanied by a standing ovation. At the back, where the RCMP members are clustered, John notices no one is standing or clapping. Despite the cheering crowd, John feels angry and dumb. *Those jerks ruin everything.*

After the party, RCMP Inspector Pat McCloskey pays John a visit at the ME office back in Halifax. John really likes McCloskey. He feels they always get on well. McCloskey is a problem solver and an excellent PR man. John has relied on him on many occasions.

"Well, Doc, we're trying to get a Commissioner's Commendation for the troops who worked on Swissair, and we could use your endorsement."

"Don't count on me. I'm not in it." John doesn't take a second to think. A valve for his frustration and anger is in front of him, so he opens it.

"Well, I suppose I can understand your feelings, Doc, but it never hurts to ask." McCloskey accepts the refusal with diplomacy and doesn't try to push.

Years later, John will view this as a personal low point, and wish he'd taken the time to think about it a little more. He's angry with a few guys, and he lets that overshadow all of the other solid and satisfying relationships he has with many RCMP officers. McCloskey, sitting right in front of him, is one of those men.

On December 21st, the annual *Maclean's* Honour Roll edition of the Canadian weekly news magazine hits the stands. John is one of the twelve people singled out for the award. The magazine carries an intimate interview with him. The piece starts with John in his living room, drinking wine and admiring the view from the large window framing the water and shoreline across the bay. John talks about his feelings. That's what they want from him now. It's the way he is different from what is expected, the way he wept with the families while the other officials quoted rules. His response to the tragedy has been an enduring headline for the news.

The article brings a fresh round of correspondence to the ME's office in Halifax. It goes far beyond thank-you letters from the families and words of support from friends. All kinds of people from John's past, including his childhood, reach out to him. The people of Nova Scotia tell John how proud he has made them feel. Medical and legal professionals send letters of thanks. After a lifetime of hiding his feelings in order to succeed, it is an emotional outpouring that finally wins him the esteem he has so dearly coveted.

Outside his office one day as John heads into work, he meets up with a colleague in the parking lot. She's a doctor at the hospital.

"I want you to know what a wonderful thing you've done for the profession," she says. "You've really shown everyone how medical professionals can have a great deal of humanity."

The comment means the world to him considering the many struggles he's having with various professional men in his line of duty. John is a hero to some and a villain to others. Relations with the RCMP are completely buggered. People he works beside, like Linda and Gordon, think he needs special handling. Jessica and Kimberly are on the other side of a pit of parenting mistakes, and he doesn't even want to try and jump across. But to another, new set of people, John is a hero. And those who know him and love him, despite his overcompensating ego, are swelling with pride. The world is seeing him as they do—a man with a heart big enough to match his head.

* * *

The week before Christmas, back at the tin-pot morgue on the side of Hangar A, Constable Chadwick's shadow-file project is nearly complete. It's a Saturday. Just as the final files go back in the cabinet, Dr. Butt arrives on the scene and the secret mission is exposed. John explodes. This is the final insult.

"What's the problem?" Rick asks a red-face Dr. Butt. Might as well get it over with. What can the old bully do to him now? Job done, and Butt isn't his boss, and this is all going to be over soon.

"You went behind my back and stole my files. You have no right to take those files!"

"They're part of the investigation, Dr. Butt." Rick maintains his veneer of courteous demeanour, but doesn't back down. He never addresses the ME by his first name. "I had them scanned. It's done."

Chadwick really wants to make notes in his flip pad as John shouts and flaps. Other people are in the room and the mood is hostile. Rick tries to keep it as civil as possible because he knows he's already won.

John then goes to David, the ME's File Technician, and demands an answer for this breach of trust and policy. But the keeper of the files says he works Monday to Friday, and what the RCMP do on the weekend isn't his responsibility. Rick tries to think of some way to save David's ass, but it's out of his hands. Butt the Bully will probably can the poor guy.

* * *

"I want you to bring David in and fire him," Dr. Butt tells Linda.

"When do you want me to do that?"

"Tomorrow. Tell him to come into the office." He's packing his bag and donning his overcoat while talking. "I won't be here and I want you to tell him he's fired."

Linda is gobsmacked. "I have no problem doing what I'm told to do," she says. "But tomorrow is Christmas Eve. He has two children, and I am not doing that to a family. You want to fire him now, you tell him."

David has been a problem. Letting the RCMP sneak out the files put the final nail in his coffin. She'd do her duty after the holidays. No need to be so mean.

Linda's boss is out of control. He's so full of himself. All this media attention is making his head so big he might not fit through the door. Linda's husband hit the nail on the head when he said, "What do people think he's doing all the time? Every time you turn on the TV, there's his kisser on there about Swissair. Who do they think is doing all the work if Butt is spending the whole day on TV?"

* * *

John flies to Calgary for Christmas. The holiday is classically over-wrought with tension and family drama. It doesn't take long for John and Jessica to exchange words.

"At least Mark knows how to be supportive," John says. 'You didn't even call me this whole time while I was working on Swissair."

"What was I supposed to do? Call you at the hangar? I thought you were busy, so I left you alone."

"I didn't get any support from my family. But Mark called. He's a good friend and he's always there for me. And, he's coming to our Christmas dinner."

"Can we be in Western Canada and not have that guy around?" Jessica has never been supportive of her father's relationship with Mark.

The winter breaks open in a furious whiteout over central Alberta. John and his daughter spend Christmas at a friend's home in Calgary. At dinner, Mark and Jessica exchange verbal blows over stuffing and gravy.

Jessica pokes at her father with the trigger finger of her unhappy childhood. "You never tell me that you're proud of me."

Mark beats her back with heavy words, "Well, maybe you haven't done anything worthy of your dad's pride and praise."

John sits silently while they fight over his affection.

Chapter Seventeen

DISCLOSURE

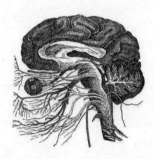

At 59 years old, John had lost much of his dark hair, and a small potbelly had grown over the buckle on his fine leather belt. His face was still round and boyish, still full of mischief when he smiled. And, for the first time since he was a teen, John was in love. He knew, logically, there was no chance. It was a fantasy. Still, his heart demanded to be heard. Integrity demanded truth. He couldn't keep pretending in the face of such an important relationship.

John was determined to tell Mark how he felt, and he had to find a way to get through the conversation without running for cover or losing his nerve. The thought of it made him sick. His heart beat against the wall of his body, as if it wanted to find a way out. The panic response flooded his nervous system with noradrenaline, creating a self-fulfilling prophecy loop of anxiety. He needed to build a trap and catch himself in it. A road trip down the Oregon coast seemed an adequate snare. In the early spring, when the magnolia trees bloom on the west coast, John left slushy Calgary to meet Mark for their getaway.

* * *

"Look, I have something to tell you."

Mark nodded, looking straight into his friend's face, ready to listen. He knew John was tense. He'd sensed it all day while they drove down the coast. They usually had such a good time on vacation—drinks, dancing, flirting with the ladies. But his buddy was in a low spot this trip. They'd had dinner and a few drinks. Time to talk it out, whatever *it* was.

Back in their room at a comfortable but no nonsense motel in Canon Beach, Oregon, John started to talk. "I'm very nervous because I know you could be upset, you could reject me ..." His voice faltered.

Mark had no idea what was going on. He waited, knowing John would get to the point eventually.

"You know how important you are to me, Mark. You've been a wonderful friend and I love you dearly. But I need to tell you, that is, I'm just letting you know ... I need to tell you that, uh ... I'm a gay man."

Mark was momentarily confounded. *Is this one of John's elaborate jokes?* No, his friend's face was ashen and stark. There was a rush of dizziness from the abrupt volte-face. Five years of friendship and he had not one clue this was coming. Mark remembered all the times they talked about women and wanting. These two images clashed. John had been married; he had two children; he even had a current long-term girlfriend—Mary. *How is this possible?* Mark eventually mustered a response. "I need to process this. I don't know what to say right now."

Mark lay awake in his bed, not far from his friend in the other bed of their double room, and listened to the waves crash against the coast. He thought about their friendship and felt betrayed. But John was, without question, a good man. He was funny, quirky, and softhearted, despite his sometimes brash, matter-of-fact approach. He was brilliant. Mark decided there was too much good to throw overboard. Somehow, he would find a way to keep this friendship.

When the two men started the seven-hour drive back to Victoria in the morning, things were still tense and quiet.

"There's only one rule going forward," Mark said, breaking the silence. "If you ever make a pass at me, our friendship is over. That's the bottom line."

"Absolutely. I would never dream of it. You've been a great friend and I felt I had to tell you. You're the first straight man I've ever told. My girls don't even know."

Mark imagined Jessica and Kimberly hearing their dad confess his long-held secret. He stifled a chuckle. "I'd really love to hear how it goes when you tell them."

John sighed heavily. "I haven't even got to that point yet. I have no idea."

The men shared a wry smile. They laughed. Slowly and carefully, the two inched their way back to an understanding of how they fit together while the highway along the curving coastline carried them home.

* * *

He'd bought the books months before. They were stacked on the coffee table, waiting to be packed. They weren't easy to track down. John had to drive out to a strip mall by the university to find a store that dealt in "that kind of thing." It was his psychiatrist, Gary Sanders, who suggested he pick up *Loving Someone Gay* by psychologist Don Clark. Since reading it, John had decided to get copies for the girls as a conversation aid for the big announcement. He called Jess to set a date.

"Hello."

"Uh, hi Jessica. It's Dad."

"Hi, Dad."

"How are things?"

"Alright. Except for work. There's this—"

John cut her off. "I'm coming to Vancouver to see you and your sister."

"Why?" she asked, her voice tightening. Jessica was 23. She had grown to be a classic beauty with large dark eyes and a brilliant smile. Both she and her sister, Kimberly, were living in Vancouver.

"I have something important to tell you, and I only want to tell you in person."

"What is it, Dad? You know I'll worry now until I find out."

"I'm not prepared to discuss it on the phone. And I want your sister to hear it when you do."

"C'mon Dad. What? Are you dying or something?"

John wanted to get off the phone. The call with Kimberly was easier. She acted like she already knew what he was flying to Vancouver to tell them.

~~ The father and his two grown daughters met for dinner at a high-end hotel in downtown Vancouver. The tall, mid-century modern building with sprawling grounds in Coal Harbour sits where the Pacific waves stroke the edge of city center and glass sky-scrapers grow faster than beach grass. In the nineties, it was still the place to see and be seen. Famous men, from professional athletes to high-rolling financiers, frequently strode through the polished stone lobby. The dining room featured two-story windows framing the sailboats on the water and the rugged north-shore mountains in the near distance.

John didn't get much of a chance to give his preamble. Jessica insisted on answers.

"What is this all about?" Jess asked before they'd ordered anything.

"Well, uhm, when I was a young boy in school—"

"Dad, what? Do you have cancer?"

"No, no."

"Are you getting remarried? Because you know we adore Mary." Jess kept on with her guesses.

"No," John replied. Her last question amused him, and he thought, *How ironic.* "I'm trying to tell you. It's just, ah, when I was young, I had feelings for boys at school. And I put that part or my-self away for a long time. Then I met Mark, and all of those feelings I'd hidden came back."

Jessica looked shocked and confused. She must have had no idea. Kim smiled. She knew.

"I've brought you these books, and I really hope you will read them." John handed each of them a copy of *Loving Someone Gay*. His hands shook a little as he carefully placed the books in front of each of them.

The girls gave their gifts a perfunctory once over and looked back to their father for further clarification.

"I'm a gay man," he said.

Kimberly turned to her sister. "You owe me a hundred bucks."

Jessica ignored her. "Why are you doing this? What's the point? Are you going to start dating men now?"

"The secret makes you angry," John replied. "I learned that from the book, and from talking with a counselor. I can't keep hiding. I feel diminished as a man when I'm in a group and people are throwing around gay slurs. No one knows enough to be polite about it for my benefit because I don't let them in on it."

Jessica went quiet. John couldn't get a read on her feelings. Perhaps she was too shocked. Perhaps she was too embarrassed to make a scene in the fancy restaurant.

Kimberly was more responsive. "I'm proud of you, Dad. I think you're being very brave."

Back in Calgary, John continued his rounds of confessions. He needed to be direct with his lover. He'd told Mary near the beginning of their relationship that dalliances with boys were part of his youth. Mary's response had been similar to the ex wife's. "So what? Don't all boys do that?"

John and Mary had been dating fairly regularly for a decade. He didn't imagine she was going to take it very well. Mary was a refined lady, and John was her dignified and successful man. They had lovely times together, and she seemed perfectly happy with the arrangement so far. There was no talk of marriage; she was a widow with daughters of her own. John liked their relationship. He enjoyed sex with women; there was no problem with that. But Mary was getting possessive and John felt she had unrealistic expectations. He needed to be honest with her.

On the Labour Day long weekend, John took Mary to a lodge in the mountains. They dined and drank, then slid into bed for an intimate encounter. He made his confession between the sheets after their lovemaking.

"Listen, you know, this is fine, this is all fine, but I have to tell you I'm ... I'm a gay male."

"What do you mean, *gay*?" Mary sat up, instantly shocked.

"I've had experiences with boys and young men in my youth." Considering he'd told her about his school days and his youthful encounters, in his mind, it wasn't right that she was feigning complete ignorance at this point. It wasn't an issue for him that they were both naked in bed together.

Mary pulled away. "Are you trying to relive your youth?" She wasn't absorbing it. "Is this about Mark?"

"We're friends, that's all. But I do love him."

Mary started to cry. John did his best to console her. He was patient. He tried to be kind.

"What am I to say to our friends when they ask about you? Is there even a place for me in your life?" Mary was a cascade of questions.

Slowly they progressed, point by point. There was nowhere else to go. There was nothing else to do. It was another trap set by John to force them both through the difficult conversation.

"You probably would have left me for someone younger anyway," she said, adopting a fatalistic tack. Disbelief and denial gave way to anger and depression.

"I'd never have made it through this last dark year without you." John tried to comfort her.

"I sure hope I don't see you parading around Seattle in a pair of diapers."

John had to laugh at Mary casting him in the gay pride parade. "I'm the same person. There's no dignity without honesty. I found I had to tell you."

Mary's tears continued. John pulled her to his chest and wrapped his arms around her slender body. They held one another through the night, talking through Mary's feelings while she cried. She did not understand.

Mary went to her doctor and had herself tested for HIV. In the early nineties, AIDS still had a strangle hold on the media and stories of the epidemic swirled constantly. It was stigmatized as a disease of gay men and drug addicts. Then, Mary divulged the contents of John's confession. She told her daughter, then her best friend, who told her mother, who told others, and Pandora's box flew open. John was mad at her, but she wasn't the kind of person to keep it all inside like he had.

She went to a few support group meetings but she thought counseling was a waste of money. Mary preferred plane tickets and holidays, thank you very much. Off to a new place with a new perspective to get over one's troubles, reminiscent of bygone days when Victorian fathers sent their daughters off to the Continent as a cure for depression, or loving the wrong man.

After the big announcement in bed, Mary continued to adorn John's arm, despite her sadness and disappointment. The intertwined parts of their lives fit together too nicely. That was hard to find, perhaps even harder for a woman in middle age. They were close and dear and more than lovers, but lovers no more.

After telling Mark, Mary, and the girls, John felt he'd made a good start. Sessions with Dr. Sanders continued, and John was on the road to recovering his self-esteem. But that letter to his first love, Alex—the letter full of all the secrets he'd spent years keeping hidden, the one confessing his love and his sexuality—sat burning in his bedside table. He had to follow through with it, despite his psychiatrist's suggestion that he need not put it in the mail.

It didn't take long to find Alex. John kept tabs on his general whereabouts through their mutual friends from Alberta. He stuffed the letter in an envelope marked *Private and Confidential: For Your Eyes Only*, then put it in a larger courier pouch and sent it off. At least, if Alex knew how he really felt, there was some chance of a reconciliation of sorts, or perhaps an end to the fixation.

Dinner parties at the buddy's house continued, though John and his friend hadn't repeated their performance in the back of the cab that night after dinner. There were always a few gay men at the table. After exposing his true self, John felt a new sense of possibility, and he took home a lover from the soirée. He was learning to let himself out.

During that same year, 1993, Pathfinder Forum Consulting Inc. had gained momentum. John went to Halifax at the behest of the Nova Scotia government to consult on an explosive case involving the death of a teenage boy. The boy, age seventeen, had died under suspicious circumstances at a bush party.

The body was found in a gully, lying in a small stream, two days after the boy went missing. Police had raided the bush party two nights prior, and, according to witnesses, the boy fled on foot with his fellow partygoers. Here, the accounts of events diverged. The boy's family and friends felt there was evidence of foul play by the local police. Law enforcement officials insisted he was never in their custody. Tragedy became a conspiracy in a matter of days.

The original examination pointed to a possible drowning, due to congestion in the lungs. At the first autopsy, pulmonary emphysema was suggested as cause of death—a conclusion that satisfied no one. A subsequent review of the findings at an inquest five months later provided new interpretations. The boy had drowned. No signs of physical abuse at the hands of police were outlined in medical reports during the investigation.

The boy's father had run down the embankment and clutched his son's body to his chest shortly after the remains were found. The death scene had been tainted. Descriptions of the boy's remains varied wildly. Rumours of police brutality, fueled by ever-changing witness accounts, were not put to rest by the review, and the family continued their cry for justice.

Gordon Gillis, the new Deputy Minister of Justice, inherited the problem. The parents were still adamant, still insisting their son had died as a result of foul play, and the government was in cahoots with the RCMP on a cover up. In 1993, at the suggestion of Wayne Cochrane, a senior lawyer with the Justice Department, Gillis reached out to Pathfinder Forum, and the professionally scrupulous Dr. Butt.

John had fond memories of Nova Scotia from his Navy days. He welcomed the chance to visit again, despite the gruesome work of exhuming a corpse. It wasn't the first time John had acted as consultant for the Nova Scotia Government. Their Office of the Chief Medical Examiner was in disarray.

John already felt a strong connection to the eastern shores. Over the years, he'd been invited to lecture on forensic pathology at Dalhousie, the prestigious university in Halifax. He remembered quaint drives down the south shore, past fishing villages with saltbox houses and inviting rows of brightly painted Adirondack chairs. In his mind's eye, Nova Scotia was all sunshine, friendly folks, and ships on the water.

Maybe this simpler life was what he needed in his later years. Maybe Nova Scotia was the perfect place to redeem himself by rebuilding the flagging Office of the Chief Medical Examiner. Then he'd retire and spend his golden years with boats and dogs and a house on the sea. But Nova Scotia didn't have the kind of resources he'd come to expect in Alberta. He wondered if they had enough money to lure him across the country.

"If we can make a deal, I'll come," he told Cochrane. It took a bit of time, but Cochrane and Deputy Minister Gordon Gillis made John an offer he did not refuse. Dr. Butt was ready to start as Nova Scotia's Chief ME in the winter of 1995-96, when the contract with Nova Scotia's outgoing Chief ME was set to expire.

At his last session with Dr. Sanders, John told the psychiatrist how helpful the counseling had been, and how much hope he had for a better future on the east coast. They sat in Sanders' new home office, a much cozier environment than the beige institutional room where they had started four years prior.

As a parting gift, the psychiatrist presented John with one of the most important compliments he'd ever received. "You've accomplished an enormous amount. You should be proud of yourself."

They were words he'd been yearning for all his life.

Chapter Eighteen

LOST AND FOUND

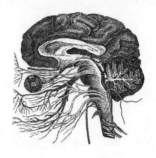

"TELL ME EXACTLY what's happened so far." Constable Rick Chadwick is on the phone with the Artifacts Custodian at the truncated Shearwater morgue. Chadwick, now stationed at his detachment office in Tantallon, doesn't spend every day at Shearwater anymore, but he's still the RCMP officer for the morgue operation attached to the side of Hangar A. And every time a problem arises, his phone lights up.

"I told Dr. Butt, 'I've got all these things catalogued where they need to stay and it looks like you're moving them.' And he said, 'Yep, I'm taking some of them to a forensic dentist who wants to examine them.' What do I do?" The Artifacts Officer sounds exasperated and confused.

"Stop him! Don't let him out of there." Rick can't believe the nerve of John Butt.

"I can't arrest this old guy. I tried to tell him that he can't take them, but he says they're his."

"Let me talk to him." Rick fumes for a few minutes on hold while the tech tries to get Dr. Butt on the phone.

"He won't come to the phone."

"You need to document the numbers of everything he's taken out of there so we can cover our asses. And try to plead with him." *Isn't this special?* Rick thinks. *Another merry go round with Dr. Butt's ego.*

Moments later, the custodian calls again. "I've got all the details written down. But he wouldn't listen to me. He just put it all in the back of his Jeep and drove away."

Chadwick calls his boss, who calls his boss, and the doctor's supposed infraction runs up the flagpole of command, where it reaches Deputy Minister Gillis. He doesn't want to make a fuss about it. As far as Gillis is concerned, Butt has jurisdiction over the examination of remains, and whatever that examination requires. No one at the top wants to make a fuss about it, so Rick has to let it drop.

When Chadwick next has a face to face with his adversary, he can't help himself. "You do realize I tried to stop you from taking the remains out of there, because if we lose control, we lose the integrity of the evidence."

"They're mine," the Chief ME says.

That's all Butt ever says: mine, mine, mine! Up to this point, Rick has tried to maintain a surface deference, but he's losing it. "I understand, Dr. Butt, how this investigation is yours," he says, and the words fall from his mouth heavy with sarcasm. "But you have a job to do, and so do I."

Two weeks later, Chadwick's fears are realized. "Remember that little thing we had about the remains taken out of Shearwater and to a dentist?" Rick's boss asks him.

"Yep."

"Well, they're missing."

Chadwick only gets a second to feel righteous before the proverbial pile of shit lands in his lap.

"I want you there on the scene and I want you to conduct the investigation," the commander informs Rick. "Come to a meeting tonight over at the Minister's office in Halifax around eight o'clock."

The constable pushes his frustration down and steps up to the task at hand. "Yes, Sir."

Their conversation ends with a few satisfying words from the brass. "What goes around comes around."

The scene at the Justice Minister's office is tense. Dr. Butt sits at the far end of a large boardroom table with his head in his hands.

Rick is almost embarrassed for the guy. *Geeze, is he crying again? He is! Special.*

The RCMP top brass, Gordon Gillis, and key staff members from the hospital are seated around the table with the Chief ME. The forensic dentist explains that he went down to get the remains from the freezer in the hospital morgue, where he'd left them, and they were gone. The hospital administrator informs the inquiry that the janitor who cleans out the freezers thought the remains were for disposal because they were in the disposal freezer.

Rick makes notes in his flip pad while the discussion continues. Old Butt doesn't look at him. Not even a glance.

After the meeting, Chadwick and the forensic dentist head down to the lab and do a walk through of what was put where. There are two freezers, one for specimens in progress, and one for remains ready for disposal. It doesn't take long to discover they were sent to the incinerator. Chadwick races up to Sydney, four hours northeast of Halifax, where the incinerator is located, but it's too late. The remains had been destroyed only hours before.

* * *

John meets with a communications officer from the Justice Department, the hospital administration, members of the RCMP, and Gordon Gillis to decide on a course of action. They don't know whose body parts were lost or what religion they may have affronted by accidentally mingling and cremating those remains. All of the victims have been identified, but it could become a public relations nightmare.

At some point, John makes up his mind. "I'm going to write to all the family members and apologize."

There's a moment of stunned silence. The hospital people try to pedal him back, "Oh no, it was just a glitch. There's got to be a better way to deal with this."

"There's not going to be any cover-up on my watch. These families deserve to know." John states emphatically. This is the Medical Examiner's ball to carry, and Gillis supports the idea. It's terrible what they've all been through. From the beginning of this ordeal, honesty has been the only real life raft for John. Facing that sea of sorrowful faces at the Lord Nelson Hotel when the families had gathered to hear the worst news has greatly influenced Dr. Butt. The families' desperate hunger for detail is like a truth serum that blocks any attempts to spare feelings by sparing information. Integrity is key, and truthfulness is a requirement.

Chadwick calls John after hearing of his insistence to write every family member. Rick seems almost conciliatory. "Geeze, man. That's brutal." For a moment, the adversaries stand together on the moral high ground.

~ John slumps through the gloomy months of winter into spring. Gillis is practically begging him to sign another four-year contract, but there's no way. It's over. The Swissair operation lifted John's sails on the eastern seaboard for several months, but that's past. He can't sit through any more claustrophobic winters leading a tiny operation in a grungy office. He can't go back to thin budgets and thick heads. And he'll never forgive them for what they did last year with that wrongful death suit. If it weren't for Swissair, he'd have left months ago.

John is plagued with a series of nitpicking issues. The Nova Scotia government wants a new ME facility, but the planner assigned to work on the project has a problem with the kitchenette measurements; they're over the guideline by a metre or so and it's slowed the whole project to a halt. The problem, after months of waiting, is only revealed when John calls the planner. "What's happening? I haven't heard from you."

"We have an issue with your specifications."

This kind of petty cheapness never happened in Alberta.

In spring of 1999, John receives a call from a CBC legislative reporter in Halifax. "Hi Doc, you going to be in the legislature this afternoon?"

"No. Is there some reason why I would be?"

"The minister is going to make an announcement this afternoon about Swissair, so maybe you'd like to go."

"What's the announcement about?" John can't figure out what this reporter is trying to get him to say.

"They're going to announce that they've recovered all the operating costs for the morgue from the federal government. I thought you'd be there."

Typical Nova Scotia, John thinks. Always looking for a handout from the federal government. So this is why Gillis kept telling him to keep his mouth shut and not grumble about how the RCMP stepped on his toes. They even threatened to arrest him once when he walked a family member through the room of exhibits. They're a bunch of macho bullies. Obviously Gordon wanted to keep a perfect and positive face on the operation so the big-daddy government would reward them with cash to plug the holes made much bigger by the disaster.

In May, John travels to Switzerland with a one-night stopover in NYC. Nancy, a mother who lost her daughter in the Swissair crash, invites John to stay at her place in Manhattan. She puts him up in her lost daughter's bedroom. John thinks she is awfully kind and generous to invite him into her home. Nancy drives him back to the airport the next morning and accompanies him to the first-class lounge while he awaits his flight.

The medical examiner and the grieving mother sit side-by-side, sipping cocktails and chatting. She reaches up, without flourish or hesitation, and strokes the back of his neck.

John freezes. Panic rises in his chest. He didn't expect this. He doesn't expect advances from women anymore. It's been years. He decides he's misinterpreting, and ignores the chink she's poked in his personal boundary. It must be a sign of affection for his position. She's projecting. Anyway, he'll be gone in an hour, so no sense making a scene about it now, but the interaction rattles him. The past few years in Halifax have been void of romance, and he realizes his prospects in the small town are slim. The eastern seaboard is proving much less ideal than originally perceived in his Navy days.

Gloomy skies and the pervasive underdog attitude aside, John finds no fault with the friendly nature of the people in Nova Scotia. When he hears of Robert Conrad, the fisherman who pulled an infant's body from the water shortly after the crash, he has to meet the man. Bob is a leader in his community. He's an educated and spiritual man. John is particularly moved. He contacts the Conrads and invites them to dinner in his saltbox house on the cliff.

Invitations for speaking engagements flood the Medical Examiner's inbox. Other provincial governments are eager to hear the details of Nova Scotia's disaster response, and John is willing to oblige. By spring, John is travelling a good deal. He is invited to speak at large-scale functions, and offered a fee for his presentations. The tears arrive with the remembrances when he gives these talks. How can he possibly explain it to those who don't know?

While he travels, John checks in with the home office regularly. Linda answers the phone at 4:25 p.m., five minutes before her day is set to end. "Hi Dr. Butt," she says straight away.

"How did you know it was me?"

"Because you're calling to see if I'm working!"

"No. I am not."

Before he can get on with his question and answer session, Linda starts with her own set of interrogation points. "What are you keeping from me?"

"What? I'm not keeping—"

She cuts in. "You're making all these plans to retire. You didn't tell me."

"What are you talking about?"

"Here, it says in the paper that you're turning sixty-five this September, and after the Swissair memorial, you're going to retire!"

John does his best to mollify Linda, and tells her it's a mistake. He doesn't want everyone knowing he's leaving. Once the news gets out, he'll lose all the pull he has left. Getting anything done over the next few months will be impossible. Poor Linda, though, he doesn't like to lie to her. She's going to be upset when she finds out.

* * *

Bob Conrad has heard a great deal about the inspiring man at the top of the bay. He's never met Dr. Butt, though the Wilkins have said so many wonderful things. The Chief Medical Examiner has been on TV and the radio a good deal, always full of compassion and comforting words. After this past winter with the tuna fishery shut down and the hard work of retaking the bay, both in a literal and spiritual sense, Bob is low. He still has dreams and flashbacks triggered by smells or certain hymns. An evening with a local hero is just what the doctor ordered. Bob and his wife, Peggy, are thrilled with the invitation.

John makes a soufflé. It rises and holds, impressing the guests. Bob observes his host's skill and feels the ease in the room. John seems completely relaxed. He treats his new guests like old friends, and insists they use his first name. Ben and Deputy, the golden retrievers, laze on the floor like decadent carpets.

After the other guests leave, the Conrads sit next to the marble fireplace in the living room. Bob admires the view across the bay from the picture window. It's a high perspective, different from the sea-level outlook through the sliding glass doors at the back of his house near the mouth of the bay. There's more of everything from up here.

Once they've settled, John begins. "I want to tell you about the little boy whose body you recovered." The room is quiet as the mood shifts from refined luxury to reflective reverence. Orange flames dance on the wood in the hearth and warm light flickers over serious faces. "He was barely more than a year old, from Louisiana." John goes on to tell them about the child's family and what an important thing Bob had done for them.

The Medical Examiner's speech forces the fisherman back to that dark, wet night and he tries to imagine a profession in corpses and tragedy. *What kind of make-up does it take to do this man's job? What a privilege it is to be sitting here, guests of honour, in Dr. Butt's living room.*

In years to come, and thanks to Dr. Butt, Bob will meet the child's family. The boy's grandfather will fold the fisherman's hands in his own and say, "I want to touch the hands that last touched my grandchild." In this moment, Bob will feel all the grace and gratitude he first experienced that night on the water, and he'll know again why he was there.

* * *

Three memorial sites are chosen: Whalesback, a section of crown land on the coastline just outside of Peggy's Cove; Bayswater, another piece of coastal crown land on a hill across the bay, close to Blandford; and at the exact longitude and latitude of the crash site, as marked on official maps.

At four in the morning on September 1st, Ron Jeppesen, Supervisor of Construction Trade Services for Nova Scotia Public Works, drives a truck loaded with coppery bronze coffins to the memorial site at Bayswater. It's the day before the one-year anniversary. Over the course of the past year, Ron's focus has switched from morgue building to memorial construction. The Whalesback Memorial is a wonder of granite. One massive, grey boulder sliced precisely in half with the exposed surfaces polished to a sheen. The two halves sit at right angles on a platform of granite tiles, framing a view of the sea. Their smooth fronts are inscribed with poignant words of dedication, including an aptly poetic epitaph: *They have been joined to the sea and sky. May they rest in peace.* One rock faces the crash site, and the other faces the interment site across the bay. Three notches in one half of the large stone at Whalesback echo three large stone columns erected at the memorial site in Bayswater.

Ron pulls up to the Bayswater site in the dark. Each casket in the back of his truck had a code number and a specific place in the burial plan. Three long, deep trenches have been dug just up the hill, at the top of a woodsy path where evergreen trees give way to a small field of gravel. Another granite tiled platform holds a wall of polished stone, a giant's final resting place, inscribed with the names of all those who were lost, save two. The omissions are at the insistence of family members who were not happy with the memorial and interment of intermingled, unidentified remains. Waves of salt spray fill the air with the scent of another dimension. Repetition marks time as water crashes forward and sweeps away again. The view out to sea is akin to a starry sky at night, vast and humbling.

When Ron asked his coworkers for pallbearers to help with the interment, the response was overwhelming. He had to develop criteria for choosing whose offer of help to accept. In the end, only those who had worked on the Swissair recovery were chosen for the job.

The volunteer workers arrive at the interment site before first light the day before the ceremony. Ron rigs tarps overhead, stringing them tree-to-tree, to protect the private ceremony from the overhead eyes of the media. Helicopters buzz the site after sunrise. A bright orange fence encircles the three long crypts and the three stone pillars stand guard. Toward the water, at the edge of the clearing, a tiered, plywood grandstand waits for the crowd of mourners to witness. But not today—today, all but three of the coffins will be carefully laid to rest. It will take the entire day to complete. Despite the lack of audience, the ceremony is carefully conducted.

Men in matching short-sleeved dress shirts and sky blue hard hats form a semi-circle with their green wheelbarrows around the mound of displaced earth beside the trenches. They hold shovels, straight and still, waiting with reverence for the burials to begin. More volunteers, with matching long-sleeve dress shirts and black ties, act as pallbearers. Religious leaders from various denominations commit the coffins to the ground. Words from the different scriptures meld into the same meaning. Death comes for us all, yet we must keep living.

At noon, workers break for lunch. They sit on picnic tables in the park next to the burial site, munching on sandwiches and fruit under a splendorous sun. Camaraderie colours the afternoon. Despite the sombre task, the mood is pleasant and calm. This day marks the beginning of an end to the deep effect this tragedy has had on their lives. They've survived.

The men in blue quietly roll loads of dirt to the edge of the trench and slide it down over the caskets after they are lowered. Each coffin must be packed tightly before the next, and the next, or a hollow will form in the ground above the burial site. The majority of domed caskets, containing approximately 100 pounds of unidentified human remains apiece, are laid to rest. Three coffins wait, placed modestly over the hole left to accept them, for the hundreds of people to arrive the following day.

On September 2, 1999, the Nova Scotia government hosts an elaborate interment, and the dedication of two distinct memorials in commemoration of those who perished near the mouth of St. Margaret's Bay one year earlier. The sun is a glowing ember on the horizon when the volunteers return to the interment site at Bayswater for day two. Busloads of mourners gather on the plywood grandstand with the sound and smell of the sea at their backs.

Just before the men of God take to the podium, Ron spies puffs of smoke wafting up through the trees. *Oh no,* he thinks, *the generator must be on fire.* It takes a good deal of power to supply the PA system they've set up for the day. The generator is so noisy that they did their best to muffle the sound by burying the machine in layers of soundproofing. Ron is sure it's caught fire. Then the Catholic priest emerges from the wood waving his censer to and fro, the smoke from the incense making zigzags in the air. Relief washes over Ron.

One by one, the three remaining burnished coffins are lowered below ground. Green plastic grass frames the opening of the crypt. Everything is clean, polished, and perfectly placed. In death, we cling to order, hoping to stay in control. As each casket slips below the surface, the holy men take turns committing the remains to the earth with inclusive words of comfort and praise.

* * *

After the ceremony at Bayswater, hundreds of attendees are bussed around the horseshoe shore to the memorial at Whalesback. Bob Conrad waits nervously for the second ceremony to begin. The local fishermen who braved the weather and the dark sea hoping to offer salvation on the night of the crash have asked Bob to represent them with a flower gesture. The fisheries have suffered, along with his fellow fishermen. Bob rehearses his part in his mind. The distraction of practice pulls him from the solemnity of the service and he wishes he could just focus on the meaning of the day, not where to put this red rose.

When the cue is given, Bob walks in a procession through the thirty-metre, winding trail that leads from the road to the memorial site. David and Janet Wilkins, along with hundreds of family members, friends, workers, and volunteers from the Swissair disaster stand along the walkway. Bob passes them with head bowed. So much has happened in the past few months, so much healing for himself and his community. This service will hopefully provide an opportunity for the locals of St. Margaret's Bay to commemorate the tragedy and move on with life. Healing is important for so many reasons, from spiritual to financial.

When Bob reaches the severed-boulder memorial, he places the rose gently on the rocks. In the middle of the bay, *HMCS Halifax* acts a sentinel. The view beyond the granite coastline offers calm waters sparkling in the sunlight. It's a completely different day from one year ago. The sky is large and the sun generous. It's a perfect Nova Scotia afternoon.

CHAPTER NINETEEN

WRONGFUL DEATH

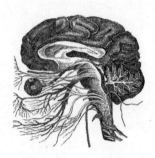

ON THE 27ᵀᴴ of December, 1994, approximately one year before John took up residence in Nova Scotia, and four years before Swissair 111 fell from the sky above Peggy's Cove and shattered the lives of so many, he had his first taste of winter in the maritime province. At that time, he might have noted the claustrophobia-inducing low sky, or the biting cold, had he not been busy with a case involving a badly decomposed corpse and the distraught, disenfranchised parents of the deceased, still looking for answers in the death of their son currently designated as drowning.

They met for the first time on a frigid night at the Delta Hotel in Sydney, a small city of 30,000 snugged into a giant coastal crag on the eastern side of Cape Breton Island.

The parents brought hired guns: another pathologist, whom John liked and respected; and some cheap cop turned PI from the states, whom John didn't think worthy of the role. It was a bit heartbreaking to see these people paying money hoping to find a reason for their son's death. Dr. Butt tried his best to reassure the family that fairness was paramount in his work. He put families, and the answers they yearned for, at the top of his priority list. He explained his role as an independent medical investigator, and walked them through the steps about to be undertaken in an effort to answer their questions.

The following day, the remains were exhumed. The body and casket had been interred in a watery grave for four years. The autopsy took place at the Glace Bay Hospital. Dr. Butt looked on as police photographers documented the casket deteriorating around the disarticulating body. It was difficult to discern specific structures in the pile of dissolving tissue and bones. Fortunately, the organs, held in a treated black plastic bag and stashed in the body cavity after the previous autopsy, were still somewhat intact. The procedure was long and grueling, and John was more than prepared to come out of it with a conclusion that didn't support the official findings thus far. Catching out a liar in the judicial process would be a triumph for a man in his position.

However, John's findings provided no additional answers for the grieving family. Dr. Butt determined the teenage boy had died of alcohol consumption, leading to risk-taking behaviour, and finally, exposure. The boy, he concluded, had fallen in the shallow stream, and lacked the capacity to right himself. The frigid overnight conditions, coupled with alcohol in the bloodstream, lowered his body temperature to the point of death. John concluded his report by stating: "The deceased has neither killed himself nor been killed."

The parents remained unsatisfied and continued to doubt the findings, insisting on collusion and cover-up. *If they only knew*, John thought, *how much tension there was between the different departments within the legal system.* The laws that govern are woven with words designed to allow for interpretation—qualifiers like "may" instead of "must" give leeway to those interpreting. In John's experience, his reading of the law often rubbed up against the RCMP's interpretation. John would have loved to prove them wrong, and finally make them apologize for something. But facts were facts, and nothing he could find pointed to wrongdoing by anyone other than the boy himself. No one was satisfied. The case, a thorn in the paw of Nova Scotia Justice, lingers to this day.

On January 7th, 1996, after accepting the offer to become the Chief ME of Nova Scotia, Dr. Butt arrived in Halifax with his two dogs and a suitcase stuffed full of clothes to start his new life.

Everything else was on a train, crossing the snow-covered country behind him. The dogs were boarded at a kennel out of town while John hunted for a home. He rented a temporary flat in the city, close to his dark little office, and walked to work day after day. The weather was gloomy, wet and cold, with a soaked grey sky bulging overhead.

In the cubist concrete building, up a short flight of cement stairs, just inside the long, two-tone teal hall, John's tiny new office with its dingy carpet and dirty windows did little to cheer him. He was used to a world-class facility of his own design, a set of laws he'd had a hand in forging, and a large team of specialists in two cities working under his authority. The NS office, including reception, files, and resource library, wasn't half the size of the waiting area with the fountain and wood benches at John's Calgary office. Coming to Halifax as the Chief ME felt like a step down, but he'd lost his prestigious position in Alberta, and he missed being on the inside.

The Nova Scotia Office of the Chief Medical Examiner had two full time staff members, and one part-time file clerk. The field investigators were RCMP Officers and local doctors located throughout the province, both largely untrained in the intricacies of death investigation. There were no standard forms used to gather data or record procedures. Often, when the Office of the Chief ME called on a doctor to attend a scene, the doctor politely declined. Samples sent to hospital labs took up to a year to return results. All of these backwoods issues seemed surmountable in the sunny days of the past summer when John negotiated his contract. He neglected to anticipate the existence of a completely different culture when it came to getting things done.

One bleak Sunday, the lonely westerner called a friend back in Calgary and cried out his regret. "I think I may have made a terrible mistake," he said, sobbing. "The winter here is incredibly gloomy." Though he blamed the weather, loneliness was the truest culprit. He missed socializing with intellectual friends at dinner parties where he could let down his guard and be real with people. A whole new town, small and chatty, lay before him, and he couldn't negotiate a way in.

Despite his dissatisfaction, John had signed a three-year contract and he had no choice but to stay and work. He slogged along through the winter, imposing new, much-needed rule with his often heavy-handed style. He hired part-time Nurse Investigators and had them work with the rural doctors and RCMP over the phone on death scene investigations in remote locations. He developed new forms for use throughout the province and streamlined systems for efficiency and accuracy. He insisted on greater cooperation from the pathology labs around the province. It was a slog, but nothing he couldn't handle after juggling the Chief Coroner position while building the Office of the Chief ME in Alberta so many years ago. This was another chance to demonstrate success and sample the sweetness of re-establishing some self-esteem.

When winter gave way to warmer weather and spring blooms, his house was finally ready to inhabit. John and the dogs moved into a saltbox on the seashore cliff in early April. Frank and Shirley next door were the first friendly neighbours who welcomed him in their home. Then he met Geoff and Jan. They shared dinners and dog love, good wine, and thrift-store road trips. Weekends with the view of the bay, good food, and friends, changed his life on the east coast. He was starting to fit in and feel at home. When his Jeep arrived, he began the daily commute between his cozy new home in Glen Haven, near the apex of sparkly St. Margaret's Bay, and his dingy office in downtown Halifax, thirty miles away. But it was bearable with his new social circle and the return of a big blue sky.

A young RCMP officer brought a cold case to the new Chief ME. John was happy to take on old files. It was, after all, the mystery that intrigued him most in his work. But he wasn't keen on the RCMP attitude. They seemed all to be looking to get a leg up and they were too arrogant to bother following the rules. This officer had taken a skull out of province to have it examined at the University of New Brunswick. John was incredulous. "That's against the law!"

"Well, I didn't know. But it's fine. It's with another doctor, a specialist, for examination."

"It doesn't matter who it's with! You can't just break the law. You don't have that kind of authority." John was fuming.

"But ... I'm a cop."

"I'm not working with the RCMP on this if you can't follow the rules." He had enough of holding his hands like a stirrup for this kid. That was it. John kicked him out.

* * *

The next morning, Linda got an early call from McCloskey, the RCMP liaison for the ME's office.

"Linda, we have a problem."

"Well, out with it, what is it?"

"Dr. Butt had a big blow-up and he's saying he won't work with us. We can't get the job done without his cooperation, you know."

Of course she knew. This new guy was stepping on more toes than a nervous boy at his first school dance.

She'd met Dr. Butt two years before he took over as Chief ME, when the government brought him out to consult on a case. He came to her office to talk to the last Chief. After Dr. Butt left, the man in charge announced his thoughts on the western doctor.

"I just don't jive with him. I don't like him."

"He seemed fine to me," Linda said calmly. "But he's gay. I'm sure of it."

"What? You can't say things like that about people!"

"I get vibes off of people. I don't care what he is, but I'm telling you, the man is gay."

After working with Dr. Butt for months, she was as sure as ever of her assessment, though he never brought it up, and neither did she. Everyone seemed to know. They talked about it when he wasn't around. The RCMP guys threw the word "gay" back and forth between themselves, a secret insult in a game of keep-away. Linda made jokes behind his back, too, but mostly at home with her husband. She didn't care that her boss was gay. He could be a real asshole, though, and making fun of him helped her cope.

There weren't any gay cops or even doctors in her world, not living as gay men, anyway. She knew why he was keeping his identity close. But Linda didn't connect Dr. Butt's cloaked sexuality with what she saw as his difficult personality. She didn't think that maybe those backroom insults left a vapour-trail of ill will that put her new boss on edge.

"You just get your men back here this afternoon and we'll talk it all out," Linda told McCloskey. She decided in the beginning that the only way to get along with Dr. Butt was to be brutally honest. So far, it was working. He usually listened to her when she scolded him.

At the meeting, Linda was able to smooth out the kinks between John and the RCMP, and she expected the row to pass without further incident. After the RCMP left, Dr. Butt called her into his office.

"What's the problem with the RCMP?" he asked.

"Well, you're asking me, so I'll tell you. And I'm going to be very honest. Nobody wants to be around you. You can't run roughshod over everybody and expect them to like you." Linda thought Dr. Butt was pretty full of himself. He had to have the best of everything and didn't seem to care for other people's needs. He had expensive clothes, a fancy watch, a pricey car, a penchant for world travel, and the attitude that he was deserving of every bit of it. Linda saw her boss as the kind of guy who always put himself first.

Dr. Butt looked stunned by Linda's words, but didn't offer a retort, so she turned and left him alone to think about what she'd said. The next morning, Butt called her back into his office.

"What's up?" she asked casually.

"I went home last night and I kept thinking about what you said, and it's true. I think you hit the nail on the head." He looked distraught, on the verge of tears. "I appreciate you telling me."

Linda was nonplussed by his admission and his emotion. "Well, you asked me. I wouldn't just say it out of the blue. You asked, so I was truthful."

"I know I'm probably embarrassing you."

"Not at all," she told him. "If you feel bad, go ahead and blubber. But if those are crocodile tears, forget it. I'm not interested."

She wasn't surprised when he started to laugh. It was just like him to be a faker.

* * *

John thought Linda was his friend. He thought she was trying to cheer him up. He appreciated her sense of humour and her forthright approach. A good dose of irreverence was just the thing to get them through the difficult times, and he was thankful for her presence in the office. She was an efficient, hard-working assistant with no-nonsense about her. John felt they had both a solid friendship and work relationship, and her opinion was important to him. He'd also hired some excellent intensive care and emergency nurses, and trained them in death investigation techniques. They became the eyes and ears of the Nova Scotia ME's office, and John's right hand. He relied on the women around him, the staunch and hardy mothers and wives, to keep the parts of his office oiled and moving. They got the job done.

The men around him weren't as easy to understand. John's almost filial obedience to his interpretation of the law, and his incessant need for decorum in following the rules of fair play, didn't fit well with the men running this maritime province. He continually ran up against cultural and financial barriers. Executing the letter of the law was expensive, and often pedantic.

In the early afternoon of November 10, 1996, two month's before John's contract with the Government of Nova Scotia began, Richard Albert Clarke died while in the care of the Nova Scotia Provincial Forensic Psychiatry Service. At the time of his death, he was a young man in his early twenties with mental health issues that made him occasionally dangerous to himself and others. His ever-changing and complicated cocktail of antipsychotic and antidepressant drugs helped him morph from an average-sized male to a hulking 340 pounds. Despite the difficulties, his parents loved him a great deal and did their best to care for him.

Approximately six years before his death, Rick had his first known psychotic episode. He heard voices with specific instructions. He lit the house on fire. The family doctor prescribed haloperidol. More than a year later, a psychiatrist assessed the troubled young man. Over the next five years, more than fifteen different medications, in varying dosages and combinations, were prescribed in attempts to stabilize Rick's temperament. In August of 1994, when he had once again been admitted to the hospital for his behaviour, a conference was held on his behalf. Mr. and Mrs. Clarke met with a dozen health care and justice professionals. All agreed. Richard needed placement in a specialized home equipped to handle his potential for violent outbursts. For myriad reasons—gaps in the system, a lack of funding, the lack of appropriate facilities—no placement ever materialized.

Richard Clarke's violent outbreaks continued for another two years with increasing frequency. Shortly after Richard was admitted for the last time to the Aberdeen Hospital's Mental Health Short Stay Unit in his hometown of New Glasgow, he attacked a nurse. She had followed Richard into his room after he was observed shouting at people in the corridor.

She sat and watched while Richard bent down to put on his shoes, muttering that he was leaving. Without warning, he grabbed the nurse, threw her down, and repeatedly punched her and banged her head against the floor. The beating continued while a fellow nurse ran for help. Then, for no reason, and as abruptly as it had started, the attack ended.

RCMP officers arrested Richard and charged him with assault. During the young man's incarceration awaiting judgment, no psych evaluation was performed, despite the location and circumstances of his arrest. At Richard's hearing, the provincial court judge remanded the young man to the Nova Scotia Hospital in Dartmouth, across the Bedford Basin inlet from downtown Halifax, and 100 miles from his parents.

In the psych ward, in a small, locked room, Richard was left to himself and the course of psychiatric drugs working their way through his blood-brain barrier. Unfortunately, his temper, perhaps exacerbated by the strange surroundings and sudden separation from the people he knew, was not easily quelled.

Three male nurses entered Rick's hospital cell to medicate him.

The patient took his pills, then threw a glass of orange juice in the face of one of the men. The three nurses struggled to restrain the obese, angry young man, then, according to their statements, left him shouting in his locked room.

Within minutes, Richard was dead.

Both the hospital and the Chief Medical Examiner's Office conducted investigations into the cause of death. Mr. and Mrs. Clarke were devastated. It seemed every step further into the healthcare system had taken them in the wrong direction. Richard was gone. They wrote a letter to the Chief Medical Examiner asking for an inquest into their son's death. By this time, Dr. Butt was in place as Chief ME for Nova Scotia. The Clarkes had taken their son to the hospital to protect others from his outbursts, but who was protecting Rick from the barrage of drugs and the system that administered them? They thought their son was reasonably healthy, despite the weight and developmental disabilities. Why had he died? Who was at fault? They wanted answers.

Dr. Ian Salathiel, a pathologist at the Health Sciences Centre in Halifax, who worked part time for the Office of the ME, conducted an autopsy on Richard Clarke's remains, but failed to find any definitive indication as to cause of death. Dr. Salathiel found signs of coronary artery disease, but the autopsy showed no evidence of myocardial infarction: Richard did not die of a heart attack. He had no severe injuries or immediately life-threatening diseases.

John told Ian they'd wait for toxicology results to come back from the lab before they went any further. But John was troubled by the lack of a clear cause. This young man was in lawful custody, and in a hospital. The government was squarely responsible for this man at the time of his death.

While he was waiting for the toxicology results, John paid a visit to the hospital where Richard died. He made an appointment with the head administrator and expected at least an exchange of information and ideas. He thought they were working toward the same goal. The reception was cool, however. John felt the woman in charge was defensive, and he left thinking she had something to hide. He wondered what the three male nurses did in those last few minutes of Rickard Clarke's life. Smothering, for example, usually left no physical evidence for a forensic pathologist.

The toxicology results showed a high level of benztropine, a drug used to counteract certain side effects of antipsychotics. For some time before his death, Richard had suffered Parkinsonian-type symptoms as a side effect of his drug cocktail. John had never seen an overdose death from benztropine before, but he couldn't deny the large dose looked suspicious, so he sought out an expert opinion. A pharmacology PhD in the department of Psychiatry at Dalhousie who specialized in psychotropic drugs justified John's suspicions. According to the expert, the amount of benztropine was high enough to potentially cause an overdose. The ME listed the immediate cause of death as Combined Drug Toxicity due to Polypharmacy and Other Significant Conditions. Richard also had clogged arteries and issues with sleep apnea, but Dr. Salathiel found no unequivocal evidence that the coronary artery disease had caused the death.

John called the Clarkes and gave them the sad news, then told them he was planning to press for a public inquiry into their son's death. The young man died in custody, of a preventable cause, and that was definitely grounds for further investigation. In Nova Scotia, only the Attorney General or the Chief Provincial Court Judge can order a public inquiry. When John took his evidence to his boss, he was asked to get another opinion on the toxicology results before he took his request to the appropriate authorities. Another specialist in Toronto sent back the same interpretation of the test results: overdose of benztropine.

John went back to his boss with the requested second opinion, and found a new participant had been added to the conversation. Wayne Cochrane, the lawyer, was already at the table. It was Cochrane who had flown to Calgary to interview and woo John for the job in Halifax. It was Cochrane who had taken the tours of the Alberta offices and talked to the staff. He knew all about John's philosophy regarding death investigation and his families-first approach. John had become increasingly suspicious of the government lawyer.

Cochrane oversaw the legal representation of the Medical Examiner's Office and the Nova Scotia Hospital, and John didn't see how they could conduct a transparent inquiry in those muddied waters.

In the spring of 1998, a year and a half after Richard Clarke died, the courts heard evidence on the cause and circumstances of his death. The Chief Medical Examiner was not called to give evidence, but Dr. Ian Salathiel, the forensic pathologist who had conducted the autopsy for the Office of the Chief ME, spent a day in a New Glasgow court defending the integrity of the Chief Medical Examiner's motivation for requesting the inquiry.

"I'll never do that again," Salathiel told John after the hearing was over.

John thought Ian was going to quit. He didn't want that to start happening again—staff dropping like flies from stress or damaged egos. "Let's go over the problem. Tell me what happened."

"The hospital's lawyer asked me if the focus of the Medical Examiner's Office was the family. They were making it sound like the Clarkes were pushing your buttons."

Ian's information was devastating to John. Though an outside lawyer had been hired to represent the NS Hospital in court, it seemed Cochrane was pulling all the levers. Of all the complaints people had about Dr. Butt, no one had questioned his ability as a forensic pathologist, or his integrity as a medical examiner. *I've been left out to fry*, John thought. *Imagine questioning my policies but not calling me in to testify?* He was livid. In that moment, John knew he wouldn't stay with the Nova Scotia Government past the end of his nearly expired contract.

The Clarke inquiry, published in July of 1998, came to nothing. The death was considered "due to complications," and faultless. The judge provided a rationale for every action that may have been perceived as an error. Essentially, Richard Albert Clarke was blamed for his own death while in custody. He was obese, an important artery was perhaps 80% blocked, he fought with his attendants and overloaded his heart's capacity to pump blood through the narrow slit remaining, he'd succumbed to an arrhythmia while the three male nurses gave him a time-out in the locked hospital room. A whole new explanation was written right into the judgment.

～ Despite the official autopsy report, drug overdose was considered an unlikely contributor. The evidence presented on toxicology was swept aside as unreliable after the doctor at the head of the Toxicology Laboratory at the QEII Health Sciences Centre in Halifax, a man in the employ of the Nova Scotia health care system, waxed poetic on the unreliability of drug levels in blood to predict death considering the weight of the deceased. Therapeutic ranges are, after all, based on averages, including average size.

If Rick hadn't presented with violent tendencies, if he hadn't gained all that weight from taking the meds trying to control his violence, if he had found a placement in a facility capable of managing his illness, if he'd been more cooperative despite his mental illness, he may have lived. The healthcare system failed Richard Albert Clarke and his family.

John told Gordon Gillis that he would not be renewing his contract when it came up in January of '99, when the current agreement was set to expire. The Deputy Minister didn't take it too well, and tried to convince John to stay, but there was no way. There was no trust left. He'd met with too much resistance trying to do the right thing while these guys cobbled it together to cover their asses.

In September of that year, just months before John's departure, a gruesome murder took John back to the small town of New Glasgow. He'd made the long drive to court on September 2nd, a rainy Wednesday, then sat waiting for hours outside the courtroom before he was called to testify. The drive home was dark and wet. The fall rain had washed the colour from the landscape. A monochrome expanse of grey water, sky, and land blurred past the car through a lacey blind of rain rivulets on the windows. John hardly noticed, remembering his last connection with New Glasgow and the suffering of Richard Clarke's parents. The trip refueled his desire to get away from this place.

At home, John tried to put his jangled nerves at ease. He walked the dogs and ate a late meal before bed. When the phone on the bed-side table rang a little before 11 p.m., he was in his pajamas. *What now?*

A woman's voice delivered unfathomable words. "I've just had a telephone call from the Halifax Rescue Coordination Centre that a plane's gone down somewhere off the Aspotogan Peninsula."

Chapter Twenty

PATHFINDER FORUM

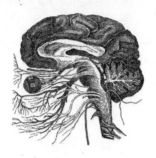

"**Swissair one eleven** heavy is declaring Pan Pan Pan. We have smoke in the cockpit ..."

Four years, fifty-seven million dollars, and thousands of labour hours later, the Transportation Safety Board issued a three hundred and thirty-eight page report on the cause of the crash. The TSB found that the entertainment system, a retrofit installed after the plane was built, had been the main contributing cause of the fire. The system's wiring had developed fatal cracks in its coating, and electric current had slipped through the breaks in the brightly-coloured plastic. Excited electrons of energy danced between the wires a few feet above the pilots' heads in the cockpit ceiling where the brain of the plane was housed. A supposedly safe silver surface on the insulation tucked around the workings turned out to be flammable, and the quick-stepping voltage ignited a fire. Within minutes, smoke flooded the cockpit and the heat raged from above, eventually melting the ceiling.

～ The time between the detection of smoke and catastrophic failure of the aircraft was approximately thirteen minutes. Both pilots were highly skilled. They knew the plane was too heavy to land without dumping fuel, so they turned away from the airport to jettison the load, hoping to circle back. As the fire consumed the wiring in the attic above the cockpit, the electrical systems failed in rapid succession.

"And we are declaring emergency now Swissair one-eleven."

The plane lost power and the pilots were flying nearly blind in the inky black night. Approximately six minutes later, the nose of the aircraft dipped slightly, imperceptibly. Human systems of proprioception and vestibular balance are not equipped to give accurate information on the feelings of flight. Before long, the angle of the vessel coupled with the forces of velocity created disastrous conditions and the plane spiralled into a nosedive toward the water. The impact collapsed the metal, crumpling the nose to the tail in a fraction of a second. Mercifully, the deaths were instant. Tragically, there was no way the plane could have landed, heavy with fuel and lacking instruments in the dark of night.

Many of the locals and the service men and women who gathered for the pointless rescue, and subsequent recovery of remains and debris, suffered from some level of post-traumatic stress disorder. RCMP members, military personnel, medical professionals, and volunteers alike, were forced to leave their posts due to stress. The victims and their families were at the epicenter of expanding concentric circles, pushing out wave after wave of heartache, while the residents and rescue workers did their best to ride the swells and stay afloat.

The findings from the TSB were hard for some to believe. The western world, whipped to a frenzy by speculative media stories, craved explanations rife with nefarious motives. Rumours that the plane had exploded from a bomb planted by terrorists or jewel thieves were hard to quash, particularly since the plane was full of important people and the hefty stash of precious stones on board was never found. But the government and the people of Nova Scotia had done their job, and it was time to put the disaster to rest.

One year after the crash, John ended his tenure as Nova Scotia's Chief Medical Examiner. He, too, was ready to put this heart wrenching time behind him. Gordon Gillis insisted he stay on the payroll until the end of the calendar year, so John kept going into the office while he was still officially employed. It was difficult to have all of the responsibility and control, then none of either. He wanted to know what was going on. John offered himself to the new Chief ME as a forensic pathologist ready to perform autopsies and write reports when requested. In classic ME style, the new doctor was having none of it. He didn't want Dr. Butt snooping around.

On January 1st of 2000, the Nova Scotia government paycheques ended. He was heading across the country to Vancouver, another coastal city with better weather and much higher price tags. He planned to work full time at his own consulting business and not take another position as a medical examiner. More and more cases were coming his way and he was developing a niche as the compassionate expert who had the experience and gravitas to challenge sitting MEs.

In the spring of 2000, John got a call from the Canadian Governor General's Office. "Have you received any official recognition for your handling of the Swissair event?" a woman asked.

He didn't mention the Maclean's Honour Roll, the Presidential Award from the Association of Psychologists of Nova Scotia, the Outstanding Service Award from the National Association of Medical Examiner's, and the Jerusalem Award from the Atlantic Jewish Council. They were wonderful to receive, but they didn't come, essentially, from his bosses.

"No," he replied.

"Nothing at all?"

"Not really."

John didn't think too much more about it. The house finally had a solid offer, and he'd put a deposit on a new-construction condo on the west side of his new city, across from a grassy park for the dogs. At the end of April, he packed to leave and arrived in Vancouver for the beginning of May. Cherry trees had dropped their blossom blankets of pale pink over the sidewalks and streets. Dogwoods and dinner-plate magnolias spread spring petals, showing coloured centers and waving stamens. Jewel-hued flowers and damp earth perfumed the air. The people on the westside streets appeared fit and affluent, but they didn't look at one another, or say hello when they passed.

Shortly after his arrival, John received an envelope from the

Office of the Governor General. He'd been singled out to receive the Order of Canada for his work as a medical examiner and educator. The thick sheet of parchment listed his major accomplishments, including his time teaching at the Canadian Police College, and his ground-breaking work on Swissair.

* * *

Rick Chadwick called Linda. "Did you hear?" he asked.

～ "Yeah, I know. I heard." Linda loved Rick and his sweetheart wife. They were the perfect couple. She liked to call them Ken and Barbie.

"We're all upset and sick about it over here. You should be side by side with him getting that award."

"Listen," Linda told Rick. "Two hundred and twenty nine people died. Who needs the Order of Canada for that?"

* * *

The awards kept coming. In 2000, John was recognized by the National Forensic Nurses' Association with a Vision Award for his Nurse Investigator program. His alma mater, the University of Alberta, honoured him with an Alumni Award of Excellence. Even the Queen gave him a medal. The cases kept coming, too, and his consulting business kept him busy flying all over the continent to give expert testimony.

John settled into life in his two-story reverse-plan condo with floor to ceiling windows in the top floor great room. High-gloss grey cabinets reached to the top on the back wall and accentuated the height of the room. A stretch of granite countertop and a chef's stainless stove with six chunky cast iron burner grates sat at the center of the kitchen. A counter bar separated the kitchen from the open dining/ living room. Expensive small appliances littered the countertops, the espresso machine fighting with the bagel-friendly chrome toaster for space and attention. Another wall was covered with a grid of bookcase, and original art adorned what walls were left. A switch-controlled gas fireplace in the corner cheered the room when the Vancouver grey coloured the walls of glass with a sense of gloomy dampness. The furniture was modern and simple, but still comfortable. The square coffee table was often piled high with magazines and newspapers. John liked to be well-read and up to date on current events.

Vancouver offered plenty of opportunities to socialize. He found ways to connect with intellectuals and successful people, often joining groups or attending lectures. He met with local literates at a quarterly dinner group, and signed up to receive the schedule of subject speakers hosted by the Vancouver Foundation at the University of British Columbia. Some of his old friends from the Navy, and his little sister Susan, lived in Vancouver. Still, he held back on romantic love. Despite Vancouver's robust gay community and open-minded residents, John kept his sexual orientation close, though not secret. There were still too many unresolved and conflicting feelings. He'd accepted that he was a gay man, but he couldn't accept what he imagined people thought of him for it, or what he thought of himself.

Shortly after his move to the west coast, John was asked to review an old case that cut close to the bone. James Lockyer, the founder of the Association in Defence of the Wrongly Convicted (AIDWYC), asked John to help prepare a report, to Minister of Justice Anne McLellan, seeking a pardon or a new trial for Stephen Truscott.

In 1966, when John was studying to become a forensic pathologist in the UK, his mentor, Professor Simpson, had flown off to give evidence for the Crown at the Supreme Court of Canada's review of the Truscott Case. In 1960, Steven Truscott, a boy of fifteen, had been convicted of murdering his schoolmate, Lynne Harper, after her body was found in the woods near their homes on the Clinton Air Force Base in Ontario. The defence recruited Professor Camps, London's other prominent pathologist and Simpson's great rival.

When Lockyer called, John remembered how he'd felt back in '66. He'd always been uneasy about his mentor's opinion of the facts in this case. Lockyer offered John a chance to help right another wrong.

After his review of the evidence, John was distraught at what his former professor had done. In John's opinion, Simpson had given false evidence. The same year he was in Canada claiming stomach content analysis was a viable means to determining time of death, he'd also been published in a forensic magazine arguing that nothing definitive regarding time of death could be determined by such analysis. John believed the only reason his former professor and friend had passionately insisted time of death was a foregone conclusion was to dupe his colleague Camps, and thrash him in front of a new audience. It was hard to accept.

The 600-page brief, prepared by lawyers James Lockyer and Phil Campbell, pointed to other possible, and arguably more viable, suspects. For example, a convicted rapist had installed electrical wiring at the victim's house shortly before she was raped and murdered. The brief went on to identify several other potential assailants, all of whom were ignored by the men investigating the crime. But Lockyer and Campbell wanted a one-two punch. They knew forensic science had advanced considerably since the original pathologist held a jar of stomach contents up to a bare light bulb and determined the victim's time of death, a crucial factor in Truscott's conviction.

After considering the brief, Minister of Justice McLellan kicked the case to retired Quebec Court of Appeal Judge, Fred Kauffman, for a formal review. Between 2000 and 2004, Kauffman heard hours of testimony behind closed doors and reviewed thousands of pages of evidence and arguments. After the review, Truscott was allowed his appeal.

A three-judge panel, sitting for the Ontario Court of Appeal, and headed by Ontario Chief Justice Roy McMurty, heard the case in January of 2006. Dr. Butt and another forensic pathologist, Dr. Knight from the UK, each echoed the other's interpretation of the evidence: damnations of Penistan's methods, and Simpson's perceived bias toward the Crown. On August 28th of 2007, the

Ontario Court of Appeal overturned Steven Truscott's original conviction and entered an acquittal. Forty-eight years after Steven's hasty arrest and trial, perhaps the most famous case of Canadian justice gone wrong, was finally over.

On September 2nd, 2008, approximately 100 people gathered at the Swissair memorial site near Bayswater where the victims' unidentified remains were interred ten years earlier. Painted, heart-shaped rocks were placed around and along the top of the granite monument, where the names of the victims were inscribed. Friends and family walked past the massive stone slab, some caressing the ridges made by the letters of their lost one's name. John stood with the group of mourners and lowered his head, eyes closed, as they fell silent in unison for a minute of shared remembrance. Ten years had passed, but he was still deeply affected by this tragedy. It had changed him. He, too, had made healing connections and knew those relationships would not exist if he had kept himself distant from the emotions and the grief.

After the ceremony, the attendees were invited to a potluck supper at the local fire station assembly hall. Across the room, John saw David Wilkins, the ophthalmologist who had lost his teenage son in the crash. He made a point to walk past David on his way out.

"I'd like to meet you in the parking lot," he said to David as he passed.

Wilkins finished his conversation and followed the doctor outside.

"You know," John said, once they were alone, "I've never told you this, but you have no idea what it meant to me when you expressed concern for me that first night at the Lord Nelson Hotel. When you came up and put your arm around my shoulder, and asked me how I was doing? It has special meaning for me. It was hard for me to believe that someone who had just lost their son would even be thinking of my welfare or how things were going for me." John was choking back tears by the time he finished speaking.

David looked surprised. "I had no idea you'd even remembered that."

"I've never forgotten it."

It felt good to share those deep and intimate feelings with David, as it had felt good to share with Bob Conrad. He admired these men, and they him. Tragedy brought them together, but something stronger was keeping them there. It was the way they acted in the face of death and destruction, the way they kept compassion up front. David and Bob were both highly religious and devout men. Though John thought little of God, he felt these two men embodied something sacred. There is no better way to esteem oneself than helping others in their darkest times. He'd kept himself detached from the emotion for the better part of his career, but the Swissair disaster forced him to see himself. When he touched the grief-stricken, he used the hands of a doctor, and it gave them enormous comfort. Their gratitude and admiration were far more important than any status symbol acquired with a title and position in public office.

Pathfinder Forum, Dr. Butt's forensic pathology consulting company, continued to thrive. He was often hired to refute the categorical claims of medical examiners and coroners who had the weight of the justice system behind their opinions. John's experience in the Canadian system made him a rare and powerful tool for defence attorneys. The work fit him perfectly. He had thought the success of power and title, and the ensuing prestige, would be his crowning glory, the final step in his quest to be a true man, to finally love himself. But he'd been wrong. When he played David to the system's Goliath, when he righted the wrongs born of power, he filled with pride. He felt satisfied with his place in the world. Any doctor, no matter their specialty, has a drive to save people. John chose to care for the grief-stricken ones left behind after difficult, even criminal deaths. His job was to find the science-supported facts and present them in a court of law, but his motivation came from the families of the victims: he cared for the living. Then, in 2009, at the age of seventy-five, John finally had the chance to save a man's life through death investigation.

* * *

Karen Bell, a hardworking woman who lived and worked in the heart of America's automobile production zone, was a friend for life. So when Danny Couch, a former work mate and friend, was arrested and jailed, she reached out to help, though they hadn't spoken in years. The friends had once been close. Danny and his wife worked at the same company as Karen and her husband, adding after-market kits to iconic cars. They had kids the same age, so it was easy to socialize. But Karen had moved away and divorced her husband, and she lost touch with Danny. Then she received a newspaper clipping from a mutual friend. Danny had been arrested for murder.

In June of 2000, a private party in Oakland County on the outskirts of Detroit spiralled out of control. When one reveller, Jack, already high on weed and buzzed on beer, snorted a thick line of cocaine, things went in the wrong direction. He began grunting wildly and crawling around on his knees. Two women at the party slipped out the door and called a few male friends to come and help deal with the situation. Danny Couch was staying with his nephew while he got himself back on his feet after splitting with his wife. When he answered the phone, and his nephew's distraught girlfriend begged for help, he rushed to assist.

By the time the women returned with reinforcements, the scene had devolved further. Susan, the hostess, was on her knees with her dress around her waist. Jack was behind her on his knees, still grunting.

"Get off me! Leave me alone!" Susan was yelling.

Two men, Rick Collar, Susan's neighbour, who had a history with Jack, and Danny, who'd never met the offending grunter, pulled Jack away from Susan and dragged him outside. Jack tried to fight back, but was easily overpowered by the two men. Once they had him on the lawn, the beating escalated. Danny punched Jack a few times, and kicked him once, but Rick punched the would-be rapist over and over. "If you ever touch Susan again, I will fucking kill you!" Rick screamed at Jack throughout the beating.

Neighbours called the police and ambulance service. One of them yelled down from a balcony at the melee, "He's had enough and I've called the police!"

Danny got into a car with the women and drove away. When he left, a fire truck and police were already on scene. According to the incident reports, Jack was still conscious, and fought the paramedics so much they had to restrain him. By the time Jack reached the emergency room at the hospital, he was dead.

Danny was back at his nephew's, sound asleep in bed, when the police broke through the door and handcuffed him. He was incredulous when they accused him of murder. "We threw that guy outside. He was fine. We called the police!" Danny was sure the cops were lying to him. During the ensuing interrogation, it became clear Jack was indeed dead. "When I left, the police and fire department were pulling into the parking lot and the guy was still yelling!"

Dr. Dragovic, the forensic pathologist who performed the autopsy on Jack's remains, found evidence of blood in the lung tissue, and ruled the death was caused by asphyxia from inhaled blood that resulted from blunt-force injury to the face. Rick and Danny were charged with murder. Dr. Dragovic took the stand and emphatically insisted the death was a homicide, pounding his fist with each word. "This man drowned in his own blood!"

A jury found Richard Collar and Daniel Couch guilty of second-degree murder after two days of deliberation. Both men were denied leave to appeal by the Michigan Court of Appeals and the Michigan Supreme Court.

But Danny was sure that his court-appointed lawyer, Raymond Correll, did not present all the facts at trial. Correll didn't even read the fire department incident report before excluding it from evidence at trial, despite Danny's request to do so. Correll seemed to feel the graphic details in the report might emphasize the effect of the beating in the jury's eyes. But the fact that Correll neglected to even read the report negated his claim. How could he know it was prejudicial if he hadn't seen its contents? Danny had tried to find another lawyer, but no one in Oakland County would take his case. The father of the deceased was a wealthy oilman who provided the County vehicles with fuel.

In prison, Danny worked tirelessly in the law library, trying to find an avenue to appeal. He needed to prove his lawyer had let him down, but it was nearly impossible from jail. Papers had to be filed, investigations launched, facts obtained and verified. He could learn the law, but he couldn't execute the necessary steps. Then Karen called. She'd moved back to their hometown, and wanted to help.

For nearly ten years, Danny worked the law books and typed up one legal document after another, often falling asleep draped over the keys, while Karen filed court documents and searched for evidence. Their strategy was simple. Who had been there that night to witness Jack's arrest? Danny knew Jack was shouting and rowdy when the beating was done, and he knew that would have been impossible if Jack was drowning in blood. When they found the Fire Department report, and read that the deceased had been intubated, with no sign of blood or obstruction in the airway, they knew they were on the right track. But presenting evidence to the court isn't as simple as finding the right piece of paper. They needed an expert with the right credentials to overcome Dr. Dragovic's official findings. Through Karen's investigations and conversations, she heard of Pathfinder Forum, and reached out to Dr. Butt in Canada.

* * *

When John read Dragovic's autopsy report, he was furious. It was lazy, sloppy work, in his opinion. John assumed the pathologist decided the cause of death, and then went looking for evidence to support it. He'd seen it before. Some medical examiners worked hard to support the official theory of the crime. They see themselves as team players, and the structure of the American system of justice not only allows for, but supports, this type of behaviour. The ME is a tool for the prosecution.

When John analyzed the Fire Department report, the hospital report, and all the other available evidence, he concluded Jack had died from excessive cocaine use. In his opinion, there wasn't nearly enough blood in the lung tissue to cause death by asphyxiation from inhalation of blood. The paramedics all reported, and later corroborated, that Jack did not have blood in his mouth or nose when they put him in the ambulance. Dragovic was wrong, and John set out to prove it.

Jack's blood alcohol level at the time of death was 0.17, with significant levels of cocaine and cocaethylene, a compound of cocaine and alcohol created by the cells in the liver, which lasts longer and is more potent than cocaine alone. Jack's heart showed evidence of a chronic thickening of the muscle, pointing again to the victim's excessive use of drugs resulting in poor health prior to the incident on the lawn. Considering the volume of drugs and alcohol consumed by the deceased on the night of his death, Dr. Butt believed Jack died from a cardio pulmonary embolism.

At the evidentiary hearing, John's interpretation infuriated Dragovic. During Dr. Butt's testimony, the Oakland County Medical Examiner repeatedly shook his head in apparent disagreement. When Dragovic took the stand, he draped himself casually over the padded chair as if to imply the ease of ownership. But the judge wasn't playing. He pressed Dragovic to explain his findings in light of the evidence presented. Once given his chance to rebut, Dragovic backpedaled, telling the court that he had not found blood in the stomach, as one might expect if an individual had so much blood in his mouth that he could not avoid inhaling it. Danny was granted a new trial on appeal.

* * *

Playing a pivotal role in freeing a young man, and essentially saving his life, had a profound effect on John. He'd become close to Karen. He'd sent her messages of support, and at the end, told her how she inspired him. "I admire your tenacity," he'd said on several occasions. But John was sad to hear that the County had pressured Danny, insisting they would try him again, with rigour. They had reputations to protect. Danny had taken a plea deal, manslaughter and time served. John knew they didn't have much money and working to get the appeal had taxed them enormously. Another trial was well beyond their financial and emotional abilities. What if they managed to convict him again, despite the evidence? At least it was over, and Danny was free.

John called Karen and told her he wanted to celebrate; he was coming to Detroit for a victory tour. She picked him up from the airport, and told him how much he looked and acted like her late father, which he took as a profound compliment, as she had clearly adored her dad.

They went to the Eastern Market and ate at a little hole in the wall called Mike's Coney Island. The couple running the eatery were obviously having a spat, and John fully enjoyed the free dinner theatre. Karen took him on tours of the automotive assembly line plants. Motion machines with moving parts were always a great favourite. They went to the Whitney, a supposedly haunted mansion with a Ghost Bar and fancy dining room named after a former inhabitant. John took great delight in exclaiming "BOO" every time it seemed appropriate. Karen laughed with delight.

On the last night of his stay, they went to an upscale restaurant where Danny's brother worked, and the better part of both families gathered to meet the man who had saved Danny. John was their hero.

CHAPTER TWENTY-ONE

CLUB DEAD

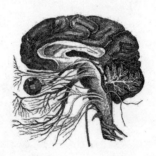

"BUT YOU SEE, being gay is just a complete social misfit for me, and I'll tell you why."

I'm sitting in my usual spot on the couch in the living room. Matt, John's beloved golden retriever, has folded himself in the cube chair opposite. It's still light out and the greenery through the window filters the low sun. John is in the kitchen fussing over tea for me. We usually have wine, but he's "on a break" from drinking, and following some austerity plan with calories in an effort to get his belly in check. His wrinkled cashmere sweater and slouchy wool trousers hint at our communal comfort. Over the past two years, John has set the tone for our exchanges with his candour and thoughtful consideration of the questions I pose. But I've yet to press him on his sex life.

"When I first understood what sexuality was in a male, I had a profound sexual relationship with a young man," he saidd. "I was thirteen and fourteen years of age. I fantasized over high-school friends and athletic men in grade eleven, twelve, through university, and still do. And that was all *secret*, that was all secret. Keeping the secret is what destroys you. If you hit yourself over the head enough times, you'll go down, you'll go underground. You're like a tent peg."

"And you were sort of keeping it a secret from yourself too?"

"Well, sure. And what happens as a result of that is a very important statement. When that happens, you cannot *be* yourself. But it has to be true that if you don't feel you can be yourself, then *they* think that there's some barrier there. That is something I truly sense with people. And so now I feel an enormous amount ... more free, though I would never go to a party of people in my peer group and start telling them that I'm gay."

Over the past two years, I've interviewed John's friends, family, and colleagues. I had to be careful what I asked. There were the people who knew, and the ones still on the other side of the barrier. Since the day he sat across from his psychiatrist and garnered permission (from himself as much as anyone) to be gay, he's been trying to dismantle the wall his subconscious had been building for fifty years.

I pressed. "There's just so little ... so much about your sexuality motivated a lot of your issues in your life. But there's so little about relationships with men that we've ever talked about."

"You're telling me! There's not much." He laughs his signature loud guffaw with a hint of evil moustache-twirling villain. It's delicious, conspiratorial, and infectious. I love how his face changes when he's happy. He looks like a twelve-year-old boy, full of mischief and excitement. Despite the joviality, I feel the churning in my stomach. This is sensitive. This is the crux of the matter.

Over the next hour and a half, we investigate the lovers of John's life, as a list. It is largely comprised of women and is surprisingly short for a man his age. He claims not to have had male lovers on the side during his marriage. He claims to have had few male lovers, mostly later in life. Considering his clearly demonstrated priorities, I lean toward believing him. The night in the taxicab with his long-time buddy was an awakening, but it didn't go anywhere. The passion stayed inside the walls of John's self-made prison for years while he focussed on his profession.

John also claims to enjoy sex with women. This has been corroborated in interviews with others. When I ask him why he doesn't consider himself bisexual, the question is met with confusion. Many of the gay men he's met and befriended are disparaging toward bisexuals, and some declare there is no such thing. I can see it's been a struggle for him to get to gay, never mind the litany of other terms for sexuality emerging from the menagerie of our individuality.

"When I fantasize, it's about men," he tells me in an attempt to answer.

Our conversations about men, passion, and love follow a path. We start with younger men. He always has a young man or two in his life. Their relationships can take many forms. Mark was the first of such young men. John's current young loves come to him through medicine, and he's been a pivotal mentor in their careers. One is now a successful doctor and the other is in med school. John helped them get there. He admires them, and though their good looks and youth may have sparked the relationship, his love for them has grown into something more meaningful. He speaks of them as a proud father might, but he's also starry eyed about them, as if they are first loves.

Then we'll talk philosophically and/or medically about sexuality and repression. We're hard pressed to deal in facts here, and pass the science-y part of it quickly. Then I press for specifics on his encounters, perhaps too timidly, and we go on segue after segue, skirting the actual sex scenes. Tidbits are offered, but there is no great love, and the closest we come to it is in the early teens with Alex. The path ends at the feet of an unrequited love from adolescence. That's where I find John's heart in waiting. He yearns for a response to the letter he sent Alex twenty years ago, but it has never arrived.

"Because I loved him so profoundly, you know, and I never talked about it. I mean I never talked about it to anybody. I couldn't even ... to go back to your question about how can you endorse yourself as a gay person, how do you come out? Well one of the things that happens is that somebody gives you permission. You know? And when somebody says to you, 'Well, maybe he was gay.' And you know being gay isn't all that bad, you think, *Well, you know, maybe I could say something to him.* That's what I did in the letter. I said it to him."

Then, out of nowhere and after decades, Alex contacts John. He leaves a message at the Pathfinder Forum office. When John tells me, he's elated, he's the excited twelve-year-old who believes anything is possible. John hasn't seen his heartthrob since the eighties.

"What did he want?" I'm trying to get to the meat of it while John spins off in what-if scenarios.

"It could happen. That would be a good way to end it. All I want is to spend one night with him, because I need to know how he thinks. It may not happen in bed. I just need to spend a day with him on my own."

"But he's still married to a woman, right? So, he didn't call to say he'd held on to your letter all these years and now wants ..."

"He wants money."

Apparently, Alex's business is suffering, and he's desperate. He tells John, "I've asked everybody else." John is not dissuaded by the nature of the request. That weary heart has jumped to life at the return of his first love. He drafts another letter to Alex, offering to give the money if Alex will come across a continent to attend John's 80th birthday party. But, unlike the first letter, he doesn't send it. He rips it up.

After a month or more of communication footsie, John and Alex speak in real time over the phone. Alex wants to talk about now, money, and his business. John wants to talk about then, and the confession/love letter.

"There are things I'd like to discuss with you," John says, willing himself to remain calm. "I'm a gay man and I feel it's important to tell you that."

The admission is met with silence.

John continues, "What about the letter I sent you in '93? Did you read it?"

Apparently, Alex had not received the letter. According to him, his wife had intercepted it, opened the inner envelope marked private & confidential, read the confession of lustful love, and burned it.

John doesn't give up. "At some point it would be good if we could talk face to face."

Alex tentatively agrees to the idea, but steers the conversation back to money. John says he'll look into his finances, and see about lending Alex a little money.

John investigates the situation and decides against entrusting the four-figure loan. He calls their mutual acquaintances in Alberta and hears how they, too, were approached for money. As much as he wants to have this man in his life, as much as he yearns for resolution and acceptance, he's come too far to pay for it. Alex, once again, fades into the past, but he'll never be gone, not for John.

It strikes me that John has not known the kind of partnership that is born of love. Many interpersonal problems that have plagued him through his professional life have foundations in this fact. He hasn't learned to trust, and forgiveness for himself, as well as others, seems especially difficult. Despite his attempts to hide it, he operates with his heart out. When you're in the company of Dr. John Butt, you know how he feels. His laugh is loud, his scoldings are horrendous (I've heard), and his compassion rings true. There is a pathological drive to do more, do better, and always do the right thing. He's like an expectant bowerbird who has built a fortress of truth and justice instead of a simple twig arch with an arrangement of colourful offerings. He hasn't had the education or benefit of a reciprocal romantic love.

My husband, Michael, and I have been invited to attend John's 80th birthday extravaganza in the British Columbia countryside near Vernon, a small summer city nestled between rolling hills lined with row upon row of well-trained grapevines, and the shores of Okanagan Lake, a heaven for house boaters and jet skiers alike. The party is a two-day affair, so we're required to find accommodation. John suggests his guests choose between one of two resort hotels in the mountains outside of town, but also supplies information for a few cheaper options, like the airport hotel. He enlists one of his handsome young assistants at Pathfinder to organize the affair, under his direction of course. We're sent links to a website with details. It's cheeky. Friday evening is "The Viewing," a cocktail reception at a local winery. Saturday we're to attend "The Service" at a private residence on the shores of Okanagan Lake.

Mike and I opt for the extravagant resort spa. I rationalize this by suggesting the affair will be high-end, and we should round out the experience in style. The resort is a shrine to Swarovski with more than three and a half million crystals festooning every aspect of the modern hilltop getaway. In our room, one wall is floor to ceiling window framing the Okanagan Valley. A large bathtub sits front and centre for maximum viewing pleasure. Blonde wood and crystal fixtures provide an uneasy modern glam. We freshen up after the four-plus-hour drive from our home in Vancouver and dress for cocktails. Then it's off to *The Viewing* in the vineyard.

The winery has an amazing vista of the valley and the lake. We're situated in an open-air space with a polished cement floor and giant girders supporting the wood and glass that soften the industrial elements of the building's design. There is a roof overhead and three open sides. Along the enclosed border is a balcony overlooking the long line of silver vats where must and yeast become wine. We make a beeline for the bar at the far side past the partygoers chatting in small pods and largely ignoring the two mature men playing their acoustic guitars in the centre of the long atrium. Servers walk by with plates of figs on liver paté and curried pork. There's a pasta bar next to the booze bar.

John's wearing a perfectly pressed blue shirt and fine grey trousers. I say hello as we sail past his pod, but I don't stop. He'll be busy holding court with old friends from far away. Mike and I are new additions and it's our duty to make inroads at this mixer.

We mingle. I spy Jessica, John's older daughter, across the room, so I take my ever-obliging husband by the hand and weave us through the small sea of minglers. When I deliver a cheerful, "Hi, Jessica." I'm met with a momentarily blank face. "I interviewed you about your dad, remember? In Calgary?"

"Oh, right. I didn't recognize you." Her facial expression hardly changes. Her lips look bigger than I remember. She's flawlessly beautiful and reminds me of a princess, even in jeans and a sweater.

I liked Jessica as soon as I met her. I've even thought if we'd met in another way, we might be friends. She brought her dog to our meeting at a chain restaurant near downtown Calgary. I was staying at a B&B around the corner and she lived close by. Interviewing her was the focus of my trip. I didn't book anything until she agreed to a meeting. We sat on the patio. She tied her giant dog, Pork, to the railing and conversed with him from time to time. She reminded me of her father, but tougher, maybe thicker skinned.

"I hate the word dysfunctional. I don't think there's such a thing as functional. It makes it sound like someone's perfect somewhere and I don't believe that's true," she told me while we talked about her dad's anger and his sexuality. She's obviously torn. She was stunned when John came out to her and her sister at the restaurant. Maybe she felt foolish for not having any inkling, while her sister congratulated him, implying she knew something Jessica didn't. The baggage seemed enormous. At the same time, Jessica expressed sadness at her father's supposed loneliness during the years of hiding. In the end, her apprehensions reminded me again of John.

"I'm amazed he wants to come out and marry his personal and professional images this way. I don't know if it's a good idea." When I asked if she'd ever known her dad to have a relationship with a man, her answer was telling. "No. I wouldn't really be interested. At this point, it would be weird."

John's younger daughter, Kimberly, is noticeably absent from the birthday affair. In a rare turn of events, Kim blew up at her father long distance on their weekly call. He'd pushed too hard, or found a hidden button, and now they were on the outs. He tried to patch it up in time for the party with an apology letter, but she clearly needed more space. Even I knew that about her.

Kimberly and I met in Ottawa at yet another chain restaurant. She was harder to read than her older sister. I didn't see much of John in her looks or demeanour. She's also beautiful, but in a different way than Jess. Kim has long, raven hair, a trim and very fit figure (she's into triathlons these days), and more obvious enhancements. She's Hollywood hot.

I dove into her dad's sexuality and asked how his coming out late in life affected her. I also asked if she knew beforehand.

"I think in life if you listen to your 'spidey senses,' and you listen enough … there were people all the along who said little things. When you're young, you maybe don't pick up on them. But I've always been a person that does, not that I wanted to. If there's an elephant in the room, I'm going to be the one to bring it out."

Kimberly distanced herself from the hurt, and perhaps the broader perspective allowed her to see the edges of her father more clearly than her sister. "He needs to be needed. It's his hole, his vacancy. It needs to be filled. But it's not our job to fill it. He needs to fill it. He never has."

I left the meeting with admiration for her insight and respect for her healthy take on the situation, but felt like I didn't get to know Kim much. She kept her distance. Fair enough, all things considered. No one really wants to discuss their family drama with a stranger, especially one intent on sharing that drama with even more strangers.

After a quick and awkward chat with Jessica at *The Viewing*, Mike and I find Mark at the pasta bar. He's happy to see me, and full of enthusiasm about life in general. His effervescence is immediately refreshing.

I first met Mark in Vancouver. We had ceviche and cocktails on a patio while we discussed his role in John's life. I asked him to describe the night at the B&B in Oregon where John confessed his feelings.

"I've never been more shocked. I didn't understand it: daughters, married, five years of friendship with not even one indication."

Both Kim and Jess have referred to the relationship between Mark and their dad as an episode of Jerry Springer. Mark says he's never, and would never, have any kind of sexual relationship with John, or any man for that matter. But the girls like to disparage the friendship nonetheless. "There's always innuendo to it," Mark told me. "And Mary would throw her two bits into it. I met her. She is a delightful woman. Just, unfortunately another victim of John's fun."

After I heard the story from John, I was curious to know if Mark had felt threatened by his unwitting role in John's coming out. Mark's response was quick and sure, like a proclamation. "Not in the least bit. Because I know who I am. I've never felt intimidated by that."

Mark has pressed John for details of his love life as well. He doesn't want his buddy to be alone. Mark is a true believer when it comes to the power of love. "I've asked him many times, even ten years ago, 'Are you looking for a boyfriend?' He said, 'I don't want some old gay guy in here.'"

I can see why John's subconscious chose Mark as an impetus for change. He is constantly and powerfully positive, as far as I can tell. He is smart, handsome, and gentlemanly. He's fit and tall. What's not to like?

After a catch up with Mark, and a few good laughs, I spy Mary in a long black gown with a black shawl draped over her shoulders. She's taken the theme to heart. We're introduced to Mary's daughter, tall and beautiful, and dressed head to toe in white. Maybe she's going for an Eastern mourning look, a pyre-at-the-river kind of thing. Mary jokes about playing along. She's always been up for adventure with John.

I first visited Mary at her apartment in Calgary during my trip to meet Jessica. I took a mixed bouquet of my favourite flowers and she made me lunch. Her apartment was rather decadent, with lots of gold leaf and soft cream carpet. There were stacks of diaries and photo albums piled up in anticipation of my visit. She read bits of her writing in response to my questions. We looked at albums.

When I pressed her on details of her love life with John (feeling like a heel), she struggled to put it in context. "I had a happy relationship with him. I knew nothing about gayness, really. I don't know if it was wishful thinking or how much of it was fantasy, him being gay. I ask myself that."

She offered to have me for supper as well, but four hours stepping slowly down memory lane was enough for one visit. I left to listen to our long tape. If I learned nothing else, it was obvious she was in love with John.

Mike and I spent the rest of our evening meeting new and intriguing guests: John's cousin from England, an appeals court judge from Alberta, John's partner in the development of a new asthma drug, and a delightful medical couple from Ireland—he's a pathologist and she's a psychiatrist. By the time we leave, I realize I've hardly spoken to John. I make a mental note to wish him a happy birthday at tomorrow's event.

The next morning, Mike and I check out the crystal-laced theme rooms in the spa after a disappointing breakfast spread of fried potatoes, bacon, eggs, and pancakes. Not what we expected. At the health spa on the main floor, there's the gently-warm rose steam room, a hotter salt room, a super-hot Finnish sauna, and a freezing ice room, among others, all with differing temperatures and stated benefits to the body and mind. The spaces are lovely, but staff is less than sparse. Towels are in short supply. We give up trying to spa ourselves to a new state of consciousness and head out to lounge around the infinity pool while the sun sails across the sky. A few hours later, after bathing in the exhibitionist bath back in our room, we're off to *The Service.*

It's a dinner party at a private residence, set outside in a terraced yard on the edge of Okanagan Lake. At the back of the house, on the first tier of grass, ten or more round tables are set with centerpieces of white spider mums and peacock feathers over Caribbean blue table clothes. Each table hosts eight white folding chairs. Bunches of balloons in various hues of blue delineate the edge of the dining area. Each seat has a gift of chocolate in a pretty box. There's a microphone and PA system set up under an overhang at the back of the house. It's sunny and warm, but not hot. Some men are in jeans, but most of the ladies wear longer dresses in shades of pastel or black. My husband is in a suit, for me. John wears a soft pink shirt with a more vibrant pink tie that barely makes it half way down his belly. He's smiling broadly while regaling a group of guests with some story or other.

Two tiers down, at the private dock wobbling in the water, I can hear Pat Bruni laughing. That's where I want to be. I've adored Pat from the first second we met at a coffee shop in Calgary. If Mark is effervescent, Pat Bruni-Job (she's married since working with John) is an ever-burning sparkler candle. She took me in her arms and hugged me like an old friend the minute we met and said hello at the entrance to the café back in Calgary. We had fattening lattés and pretended to gossip while she educated me on life. Pat had a lot of things figured out.

"Judgment can be a huge block to us learning about others. I think as much as we say we all have choices, that's way up here." Pat raised her hand, perhaps indicating the surface plane of our selves. "Really, it's what we've experienced, what our past has told us."

When we talked about John, she was filled with respect, and giggles. She talked about his practical jokes, and his stringent attention to detail. I asked her if she thought the plane crash disaster changed him. She said she knew it had. "When he was in Calgary, he did not speak to families. It was a closed door. Since Swissair, I've seen a softness that wasn't there when I worked with him. When he speaks of the families and walking into that large ballroom, it's heartfelt."

At the time I interviewed Pat, I was still under the impression that the conundrum of living in the presence of death, something we naturally recoil from, was the purpose of the work. I asked Pat how she dealt with the dead. In her answers, as in John's, the corpse barely featured. She talked about the bodies and minds of those still present. "They're going to live through it because they can feel it. It's when you don't feel it, you bring it with you, and it comes out in other ways ... Let's not go to the mind, let's go to the heart. Logic does not play a part in our grieving."

She brings me to the verge, tears welling, the reddening edges of my eyes intensifying the blue irises. I can see people get stuck there sometimes when they're talking to me. My intimacy with tears often unnerves, but Pat sees the sign as positive and pushes on. "To be in someone's presence in their darkest hours is a privilege. Because we meet them at the heart. We don't meet them in the mind. We don't meet the ego. I have learned so much about how to live life from being in the presence of death." When our meeting was up, I wanted more. I could have talked to Pat for hours.

At the party, I make my way to her, walking down the brick

path along the edge of the yard toward the water. The sun sits low, perhaps at forty-five degrees. It will set over the water as the speeches wind down after dinner. I pass the picnic table surrounded by evergreen trees and a massive weeping willow across the path. On the patio near the water's edge, I step on the over-crowded dock. It's the place to be, danger be damned. Pat is sparkling away with a bunch of people around her. She's nearly buried in a large white pouf at the end of the wiggly pontoon. Her squeal rings in my ear when she jumps up to hug me. I feel loved. She hugs Mike, too. Then she introduces us to the other members of Club Dead.

Medical school teaches medicine, and the medical side of investigation. But John had little education in death-scene management per se. The presence of the grief stricken can turn the investigative process on its head. John identified that issue early on, but he also knew he didn't want to be sopping up all that emotion himself. So he thought, *Who does that in the hospital?* The nurses do it. They hold the hands and apply the creams. They also stick in the needles and wipe the unmentionables. John had a mandate for death scene investigation when he launched the Chief ME operation in Alberta. He wanted a team of nurse medical examiner investigators, and they had to have experience in the emergency room or intensive care. Club Dead was born. The four women worked together for sixteen years attending death scenes on behalf of the Office of the Chief Medical Examiner. They still meet every three months for their quarterly laugh riot. Their intermingled lives form a heartfelt story of survival in the trenches. I'm captivated by the group.

Pat and the ladies scramble over one another to tell us their stories of hilarity-laced gore. Pat is horribly entertaining when she talks about "the one with the mice and the old lady." Apparently, of all of the things she's seen, this is the one that gets her. The corpse is in the bed, under the blankets. The police have to wait for Pat to move things, including the covers. There are tiny yet unmistakable movements under the bedspread. Pat peels back the layers of quilts and sheets. The body is covered in mice. They're eating the decaying flesh. She screams (a little unprofessionally).

At this point in Pat's story, the other members of Club Dead are at the wheezing stage of laughter. She soldiers on, shaking the image from her mind.

After the sight of the mice, the poor corpse, and screaming, Pat races to the closest cop and proceeds to climb up on him while the other officer places his hand on his sidearm, undoubtedly unsure of what is in the damn bed. Pat, committed to high-impact storytelling, imitates the climbing by grabbing her friend, and prepares to shimmy up her, monkey-style. The dock rocks from the sudden shift of weight, punctuating Pat's punch line. We are all now well beyond the wheeze, some of us are having trouble breathing, and I can hardly see through my tears.

The dinner gong calls us up to the balloon tier for food and the eulogy show. I find John before we sit to say hello and thank him for the wonderful spread. He complains briefly, as one does to a confidant, and I like it. "The photo booth guy promised he'd be here and I'm absolutely livid that he hasn't shown yet. But anyway ..." He goes on to introduce me to the group of twenty-somethings standing in a circle around him.

I ask a thin, tall, attractive young fellow with a mop of flaxen hair how he knows John. The handsome stranger doesn't have a chance to respond before John cuts in. "Oh, I love him!"

The young man's adorable, longhaired girlfriend squeals with delight. He bows his head slightly and smiles. He seems pleased with the compliment. "I love him too," he replies.

On the way back to find my husband, my table, and my surprise dinner companions, Mary hooks my arm and pulls me toward the bushes for a quick tête-à-tête. "I made some photocopies of a few photos for you."

She gives me three white pages, each with a black and white image in the center. Two photos are of John's family, one from 1954, the year he started med school, and one from 1957, when his mother's terminal prognosis became apparent. The third picture, also from 1957, is John in his Navy dress uniform. His face is obscured under the peak of the crisp hat. Rows of buttons and cord decorate the vest and jacket. He wears a bow tie and heavy, shiny shoes. His figure is tall and trim with broad shoulders and long limbs. I think of what was happening for him then. How he was so unsure of himself.

But it's the picture of the family around the Christmas tree in 1957 that I can't stop scrutinizing. Jack Butt, sitting in an armchair wearing a plaid shirt and argyle socks, is the only one who looks genuinely happy. He was still oblivious at this point, a gift from his son. John is perched side-saddle on the back of the chair with his torso swivelled to the camera. He wears the blank look of shell shock. He knows. Isobel sits on the armrest in her pearls, skirt, and pumps. She attempts a smile, but looks weary. She's known for longer than anyone. Susan crouches in front of the Christmas tree at her father's feet, wearing a white lace collar over a dark dress, and a worried expression. She knows nothing, but can feel its shadow. I take out a pen and quickly write "last Christmas with Isobel" in the white space beside the image.

There are five of us at the table where Mike and I are seated. Luckily, our dinner companions become quick friends. Ed, a long-time buddy from John's Navy days, and his two daughters, keep us entertained. Ed regales us with tales from their youth. He's wearing his Naval cap. One of Ed's daughters, Melissa, who has experience as a stand-up comedian, is the emcee for the evening. Mary might say Melissa is the pastor, if we're staying true to the conceit of a funeral. Mary is still holding the black shawl around her shoulders. I admire her commitment.

The sun is lower in the sky. It's a little before sunset when the light gets milky. Candles are lit. As dinner evolves slowly to coffee and dessert, there's a brief kerfuffle with the sound system, then Melissa takes her place at the microphone. She jokes about planning the entertainment with John. "The first sketch involved him as the doctor and me as the menopausal patient, which I found a little too close to home. And it kinda ended with me sticking eggs up my hoo haw . . ." She has to pause here and let the laughter die down. "So I didn't want to do that one."

I can detect a few distinct laughs in the cacophony, like a birder in the field. There's John, louder than most. It's a gust of noise with sneeze-like delivery. I hear Jessica occasionally let out her own brand of loud guffaw. It's high and feminine but just as committed as her father's. Above all, I hear the sunset chorus from the far end of our dinner theatre, where the ladies of Club Dead serenade us with a constant stream of giggles.

Melissa continues. "John was in London in the late '60s and he wasn't making much money. So, he took a job with this company that performed medical exams for people who were emigrating to Canada. A very proper English couple came in. John examined the wife. At the end of the exam, she said, 'Do you want me to get dressed now?' and he said, 'Well, we're not planning to spend the night together.'"

All the birds laugh again and the crowd stirs like a small flock lifting to inscribe a circle on the sky. It's the most cheerful thing. We're all in a special group of interesting people who know and care for Dr. John Butt.

No one, except John, is as entertaining as Melissa. The speeches are heartfelt but personal. The jokes are a bit too high-minded or hard to follow. Still, it's lovely, and different sections of the party laugh at different things. We're really doing choral song now. Mark mentions me, the writer, and suggests a few titles for the story of his dear friend's life. "If it's a biography, we could call it *Fancy Coffins: the John Butt Story*. If it's a kid's book, *Knock, Knock, Who's There, Not You*. But my favourite is if it's a romance novel, *Fifty Shades of Gay*."

We hit a little bump here. I've been out-ed as a biographer. They don't know I'm kind of spying on them (ugh), and John's been out-ed to those in the audience who are still in the dark about his sexuality— at least half of the guests. The party-goers offer different responses. Laughs for sure, a small handful of cheers, but also a buzz of confused chatter. In a second, we slough it off and get back to the fun.

John takes the stage. He's a little past tipsy, say, tipsy with a glow. He's ruddy and grinning. I'm nervous for him, but he seems entirely confident in the spotlight. The sun is dipping its fiery crescent edge in the lake. We are bathed in orange.

He pokes fun at himself. "I have a counter discipline in my personality. I'm humorous, but I'm also a dink."

We laugh.

He goes on, "I am known to be difficult. I don't have a problem with it, except I can't accept it." He has to let out a guffaw here. "I don't accept it. I'm a loveable person."

He talks about his friends, and gives a special nod to the cheering squad. "There are four women here that you don't know, and they are a group called the Club Dead. If you do death investigation, the issue is it's a sombre situation. But you can enjoy it and have fun at your work. These ladies tickled me to death."

We give the ladies a round of loud applause.

Then, to my surprise, John comes to the point. He does the thing he said he would never do. "I am a preacher of, I suppose, being conflicted ... I am a gay man."

This proclamation, definitively stated, in public, from the horse's mouth so to speak, is a shock. I think I hear Mary cry out a little. Maybe Jessica gasps, but she's too far away for me to be sure. Across the yard from me, the ladies of Club Dead have jumped to their feet to shout and clap.

"The best part of it is ..." John tries to finish it, but the fates take over. The handsome young stranger with the mop of blond hair breezes by as John makes his grand announcement. Passing directly in front of the microphone stand is the only avenue available to access the tables on the far side, the bar, and the portable washrooms beyond. Handsome Young Stranger plants a kiss on John's cheek as he passes, pivoting with a twirl so as not to break stride. The girlfriend's gleeful noise comes from somewhere among the circles of blue in the new twilight. The crowd cheers.

John ends his speech simply. "I'm glad that you accept me and my friends. I've had a very nice time."

Acknowledgements

So many people have supported me on this first-book journey, but three men have been pillars in the process. First, my late husband Michael Izen, who often hung over my shoulder while I typed, and cheered at the unfolding action as if he were watching a sporting event. You are always with me, Michael. Next is Dr. John Butt himself. Thank you, John, for sharing your stories as candidly as you did. And a heartfelt thank you to Michael Mirolla at Guernica Editions. I'm forever grateful to you for believing in this story and its place in the Canadian literary landscape. Thanks also to Anna van Valkenburg and Nour Abi-Nakhoul for steering the publicity and teaching me how to be a useful participant in the process. A big thank you to my editor, Gary Clairman, and another to the book designer, David Moratto. Many thanks to all the people who shared their personal stories with me to make this work as round and honest as possible.

I had a solid crew of early readers, creative writers, and supportive friends who helped me immensely: Monica Ghosh, Adrick Brock, Portai Pascuzzo, Karen Garbert, Elizabeth & Chris Wootten, Susan Broatch, Melissa & ED Mortimer, Lindsay Wong, Moira Dann, Pauline Dakin, Cathy Chilco, Robyn Huth, Perry Goldsmith, Sasha Dryden, and Karri Green-Schuermans. Crafting this story was the focus of my MFA program at the University of King's College in Halifax, and I can't thank the team of excellent mentors and leaders enough. Special thanks to Stephen Kimber and Don Sedgwick, along with my mentors, Lori A. May, David Hayes, and Lorri Neilsen Glenn. Thank you to the BC Arts Council for supporting my education goals.

Last, but always first, thank you to my daughter, Chloe, for keeping my feet on the ground, step by step.

About the Author

Gina Leola Woolsey's writing explores the highly evolved and the innately animalistic behaviours of humankind. Through story, she teases out the shared themes of our lives. Gina is an award-winning author who left her corporate job mid-life to pursue a creative career. She lives wherever the story takes her.

Printed in April 2023
by Gauvin Press,
Gatineau, Québec